James Rosenquist

James Rosenquist
Collages, Drawings, and Paintings in Process

Edited by Larry Warsh

Published by Princeton University Press
in association with No More Rulers

Published by Princeton University Press
throughout the world, excluding China
41 William Street, Princeton, New Jersey, 08540
99 Banbury Road, Oxford OX2 6JX
press.princeton.edu

In association with No More Rulers
nomorerulers.com @nomorerulers

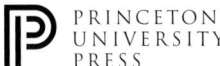 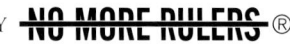

ISBN: 978-0-691-26328-1

Library of Congress Control Number: 2023948409

British Library Cataloging-in-Publication Data is available

Design by Hannah Alderfer, HHA design

Front Cover
James Rosenquist, *Sketch for Marilyn Monroe I*, 1962

Back Cover
James Rosenquist, *Marilyn Monroe I*, 1962

This book has been composed in Helvetica Neue LT Pro

Printed on acid-free paper

Printed in China

10 9 8 7 6 5 4 3 2 1

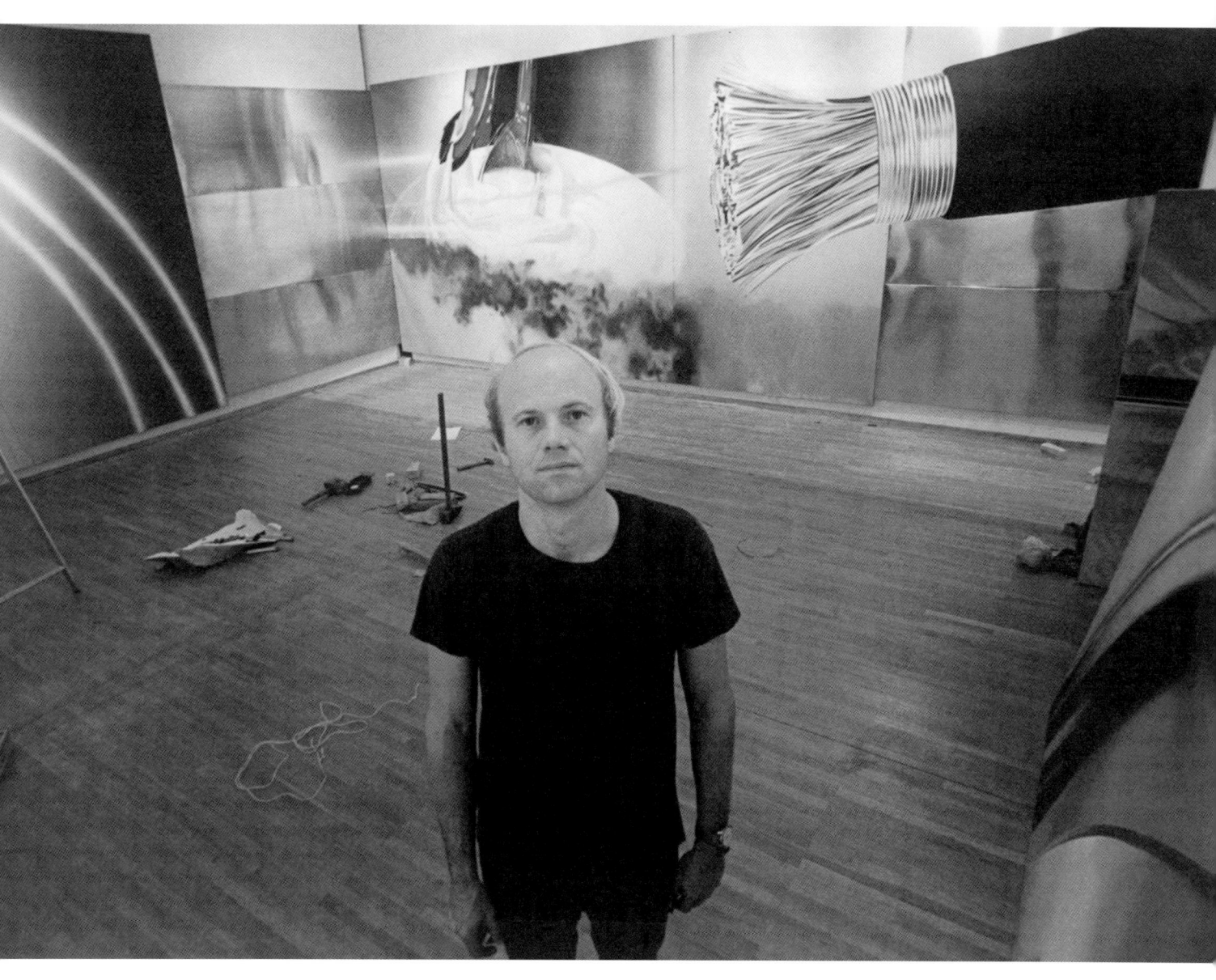

James Rosenquist installing *Horse Blinders* (1968–69), Wallraf-Richartz-Museum, Cologne, 1972. Photo by Wolf P. Prange.

Foreword

The sweeping graphic vision of Pop art icon James Rosenquist (1933–2017) might be described as a cultural mass-media mashup. Turning everyday objects—a plate of spaghetti, glossy lipstick, car tires—into monumental visual encounters, Rosenquist exerted an unmistakable, seductive gravitational pull on late 20th-century art.

His intense, fragmented compositions are immediately recognizable for their culturally charged content infused with social and political undertones, a near-existential curiosity, and a sly sense of the absurd. Best known as a painter, in the course of a six-decade career Rosenquist also experimented with sculpture, drawing, collage, and printmaking. He and his contemporaries—notably Roy Lichtenstein, Andy Warhol, and Claes Oldenburg—were prime movers in American Pop art, and their influence reverberates today.

Rosenquist grew up in the upper Midwest. The summer after high school he worked for a commercial painting contractor, painting storage tanks, grain elevators, and classic Phillips 66 signs at gas stations across the region. After studying art at the University of Minnesota, in 1955 he moved to New York City, where he attended the Art Students League on a scholarship. There, his teachers included noted artists George Grosz and Will Barnet.

With savings depleted, Rosenquist scrambled to support himself. His experience in sign-painting earned him a spot in the local painters' union, and by the age of 25 he was head painter for one of the city's leading sign companies, Artkraft Strauss. In his spare time he made his own art. In 1960, he quit his day job and took a studio in Lower Manhattan, where his neighbors included artists Ellsworth Kelly and Robert Indiana.

Rosenquist began to make paintings that drew on commercial sign-painting techniques and advertising images stripped of their usual context—or, as Sarah C. Bancroft puts it in her essay, "nonobjective 'abstract' artwork" made from "figurative imagery emptied of its original intent."

You'll see some of those early paintings in these pages. But more than that, this book takes a close look at the collages and drawings that were the foundation for many of those works.

While Rosenquist is known for outsized art, these small source works make it clear that those monumental canvases first existed on a reduced scale, fully realized and fully detailed. In this book, we can see how these small works correlate with the paintings, how the artist's ideas transfer from one to the other, and how his observations of the world become art. Hidden in plain sight, small details become evidence of Rosenquist's process, layered into the final works. Seen as the conceptual backbone for the paintings they inspired, these small source works provide extraordinary insights into Rosenquist's art and creative thought.

That's precisely what we at No More Rulers are looking to accomplish with our Sketchbook series. It's our hope that the series—and especially *James Rosenquist*—inspire visual thinking, creativity, and the inner artist in us all.

Larry Warsh
New York City

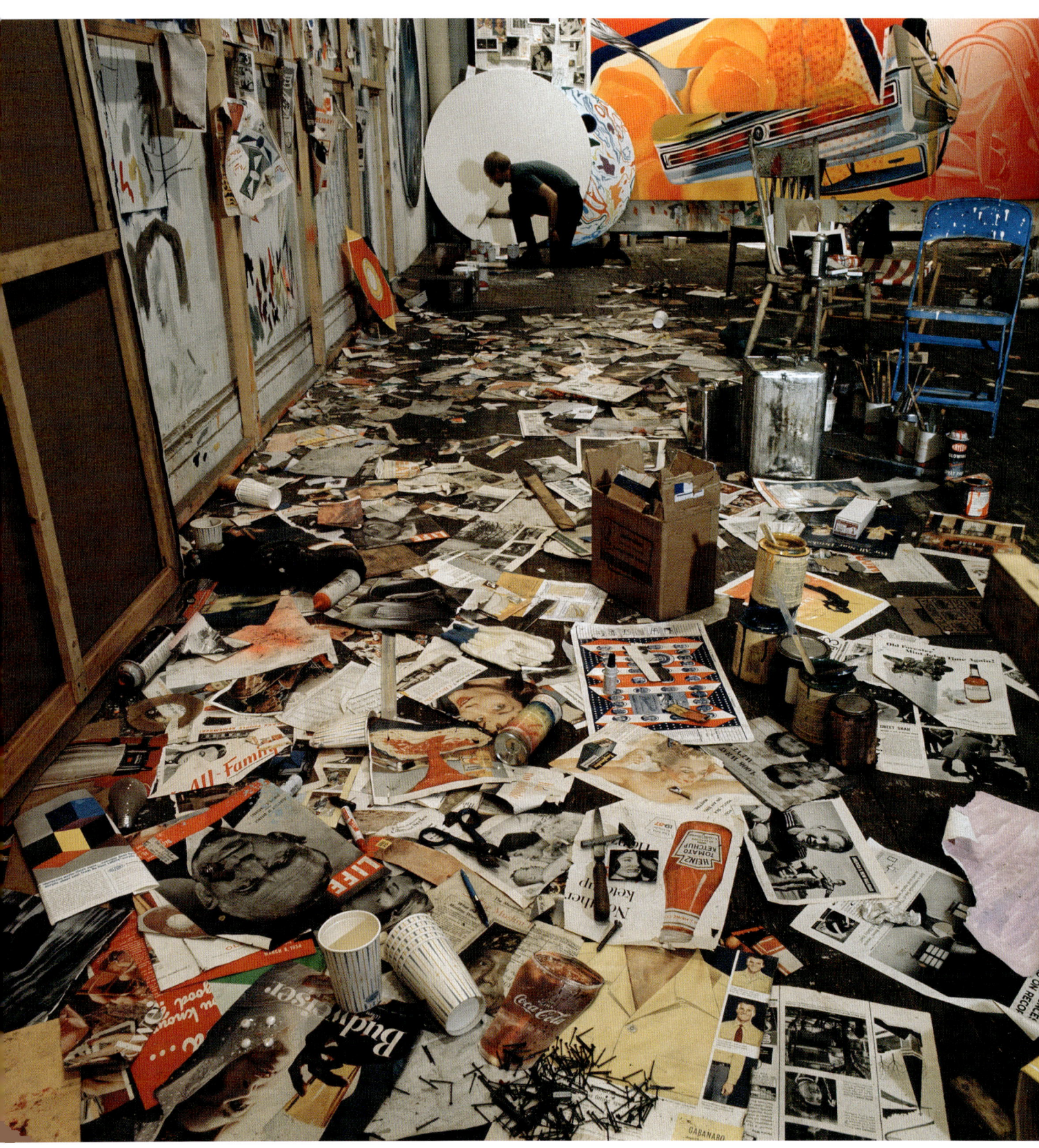

Rosenquist in his Broome Street studio, New York, 1964. Partially visible are his paintings *Bowling Ball Eclipse* (1964),
Bowling Ball Galaxie (1964), and *Lanai* (1964).
Photo Ugo Mulas © Ugo Mulas Heirs. All rights reserved.

James Rosenquist: In the Beginning

When I began using advertising imagery in my paintings it was never a question of beating advertisers at their own game. It was simply the idea of doing something that had the same force as advertising, using their techniques and bizarre imagery…. I thought, why can't I use the force of what I had been doing commercially as a billboard painter to say something of my own?

James Rosenquist[1]

The 1960s in the United States were a time of social and political transformation. As a young person in his 20s, living and working in New York City, James Rosenquist also underwent a sea change in his personal and professional life. Although he arrived in 1955 to study at the Art Students League on scholarship, within a year Rosenquist was financially compelled to support himself. He had experience as a sign painter and in 1957 joined the Local 230 of the International Brotherhood of Painters and Allied Trades union. Thus began his peripatetic day job painting billboards, theater marquees, store window backdrops, and advertising signs across the five boroughs of the city. By age 25, he was head painter for Artkraft Strauss Sign Corporation, and the following year—1960—Rosenquist was featured in the United Press International article "Billboard Painter, Local 230, Is Broadway's Biggest Painter." That year, two of his friends died after falling from scaffolding while painting signs high above the city streets. By that point, Rosenquist was creating his own works in his off-time, and he was propelled by this tragedy to commit full time to his fine art practice. He found a studio downtown in an old loft on Coenties Slip (Agnes Martin's old studio) and became part of a vibrant community of artists living and working in lower Manhattan (including Robert Rauschenberg, Claes Oldenburg, Henry Pearson, Jack Youngerman and his wife, actress Delphine Seyrig, Robert Indiana, Ellsworth Kelly, and others). It was here that Rosenquist brought elements of his commercial painting techniques into his fine art practice and charted a new course. This book features a selection of the early preparatory drawings, source collages, and paintings that embody Rosenquist's bold experiments and birth as a Pop artist.

For its billboard artists, Artkraft Strauss provided small photos and editorial layouts for the large-scale advertising signs to be painted. Working from small imagery was the norm. Rosenquist and his crew would paint out the previous advertisement, sketch a grid on the board or wall, and scale up the new imagery by hand, using the grid for reference. (He often commented that when painting a movie star's face on a billboard for a new film, for instance, the cheek was so large as to be abstract up close. You could only see it as a body part once you stepped back from the board and it came into resolution.)[2] He and his crew painted the same sign repeatedly, all over the city, the process almost rote at that point. While spending his days immersed in the visual language of advertising, Rosenquist was painting and drawing small abstractions on his own time, mostly ink gestural drawings and a few collages here and there. This would quickly change.

In his studio on Coenties Slip, Rosenquist left the commercial art world behind while continuing to quietly pick and choose images from advertisements to create new work all his own. (The images mostly came from *Life* magazine, although newspapers and photographs were also fair game). The images he selected were recognizable while not being nostalgic, most taken from magazines about a decade old. He synthesized mass advertising imagery into novel compositions stripped of original commercial intent, at once visually captivating and mentally confounding and mysterious. A handful of artists across the city—most working downtown— were also experimenting with "popular" imagery, and together they would become known as the American

---

1 James Rosenquist with David Dalton, *Painting Below Zero: Notes on a Life in Art* (New York: Knopf, 2009), pp. 88-89.
2 Rosenquist expressed this idea in conversation with the author, 2000, and in subsequent conversations.

New Realists and eventually Pop artists. (Notably, the group did not know each other for the most part, meeting instead through the galleries and curators exhibiting their work.) Each of these artists—Roy Lichtenstein, Claes Oldenburg, Andy Warhol, Tom Wesselmann, and Rosenquist, to name a handful—had a distinct style and unique background. Rosenquist personally related with the Surrealists and surrealism, and expressed a need to go "below zero" to create nonobjective "abstract" artwork using figurative imagery emptied of its original intent. This is to say, the Pop artists were not a unified group with a singular vision; rather, these artists were each using popular imagery in distinct ways that also reflected the American consumer society and the tenor of the times.

The small source collages Rosenquist created for his early Pop paintings were a discrete part of his working process, albeit not something he shared publicly. Through the collage-making process he worked out his compositions, conceptually concretizing his ideas, snipping and recombining imagery from different advertisements to make unexpected juxtapositions. These collages served as guides or roadmaps for the paintings. Holding the collage in hand or pinning it to the wall nearby, Rosenquist would scale up the imagery onto the larger canvas. It was usually a direct translation from collage to canvas, the conceptual and compositional work having been done in most cases before he picked up a brush. The preparatory drawings and collages bear notes to himself in pencil and ink, the smudges of his work in progress, color studies and decisions, reflections, or adaptations along the way. Most paintings have one source collage—the master working document, in a sense—but some larger room-scale works have several. This of course relates to the scale and size of a work that canvases all four walls of a room, and the related studies appear almost cinematic or panoramic in their disconnected, graphic-novel-like narrative quality. (For the room-scale works, Rosenquist often wished for the artwork to invade the viewer's peripheral vision, an idea he directly addressed in *Horse Blinders* [1968–69].)

For years, Rosenquist kept the collages out of the public eye. Visitors to his studio—family, friends, fellow artists, curators, gallerists, collectors—obviously saw them, but they were not exhibited for decades. Important enough to transport with him—they moved between his studios in New York City and Long Island and eventually to his studio in Florida (where he built a home and studio and worked from the late 1970s). He reportedly kept many of them in a suitcase. Others were inevitably lost in the purge of creative detritus that would ebb and flow in his studios (pages torn from magazines, images strewn across the floor, piles of paper that fed his creative process). While the source collages were of deep personal value to Rosenquist, he was secretive about his collage process, and rarely discussed it before the 2003 Guggenheim retrospective.

By the time I joined Walter Hopps on the curatorial team organizing the traveling Rosenquist retrospective for the Solomon R Guggenheim Museum, Rosenquist had exhibited a small number of the collages on only one occasion (at the Gagosian Gallery). We decided to show a much larger array of the collages in the upcoming retrospective, and it took some convincing. Eventually Rosenquist agreed, and the collages were framed for exhibition. He was surprised but ultimately unflapped by our commitment to include so many of these small-scale creations. When Rosenquist's property in Florida was overtaken by a brush fire in 2009—his studio, office, a portion of his archive, and home were destroyed by the flames—these works remained safe, hundreds of miles away from the conflagration. At the close of the exhibition, we had returned these and all of the works borrowed from the artist to his building in New York—rather than to his studio in Florida—where they remained. These small collages were stored on the ground floor of his Chambers Street building in Tribeca (miraculously making it through

Hurricane Sandy in 2012 as well), small gems that continue to captivate those who encounter them, vouchsafing his original ideas and approach to composition.

The source collages are revelatory. Never had so much of his working process been on view before the Guggenheim retrospective that traveled between 2003 and 2005 (and again nearly 20 years later for the Museum Ludwig retrospective that followed). Precious, intricate, or spare, they are microcosms of the thinking and creative process for each painting. This book provides the viewer with a focused opportunity to see and discern the collages and all their markings in tandem with select paintings from the early years. Not intended as an exhaustive guide or explanation, rather this book is an intimate and focused visual investigation.

While we know the stories behind many of these early compositions, some works remain mysterious. Rosenquist intended much of the work to operate outside of his own scope of reference, even as he had stories, personal and public, informing each one. For years, I casually and intently asked him about specific works. He shared stories that had been well worn through the telling and retelling over the years (and many of these stories are catalogued in his 2009 memoir). Ask the same questions on another day, and you might get another story, listen long enough and you might hear something completely new—eventually. For Rosenquist, the stories were not important for the viewer, although they were always relevant to his impetus for making the work.

> *Starting with* Zone *I had begun to develop an idiosyncratic visual vocabulary. Painting in black-and-white tonalities was like working with the snapshots from which I'd painted billboard images.*
> James Rosenquist [3]

Zone (1961) was one of the first Pop art paintings Rosenquist developed. The close-up view of a plump and freshly washed tomato, glistening with water drops, is juxtaposed in zigzag fashion with a woman's face, her fingers laced across her cheek. Both images are presented in grisaille—grey tones—and the painting speaks to a moment of print journalism and black-and-white photography in popular magazines at midcentury. Which "zone" of the painting is the foreground or the background? What is the relationship between the two images? Why place them together?

For Rosenquist, the absurdity of advertising was at play in this work, but it was also a play by the artist to go "below zero" to a new form of abstraction. "What attracted me in ads was the mystery, the strangeness of these bits of commercial propaganda—they were enigmas. I began thinking, what if I used generic fragments from ads and photos in *Life* magazine and juxtaposed them in different scales? And what if I made one of the images so large that close-up it would initially be difficult to recognize? Wouldn't I then have created an abstract effect using recognizable imagery? The images would be so big and collaged together so apparently arbitrarily that you wouldn't understand it at first.... In this way I could make a mysterious painting using the most banal materials. That was my initial idea about the dislocation of scale."[4] On the early grisaille paintings, Rosenquist said "It's not always easy to explain what these paintings mean. It's elusive. It may not always make literal sense—or, to put it another way, it makes sense only if you *can't* translate it into words.... People might look at them and say," God, they're awful!" or they might find them ingenious, but in the end, it's their inability to be explained that makes them so indigestible. They're odd and enigmatic....and yet I think they're some of my best work."[5]

3 Rosenquist with David Dalton, p. 102.
4 Rosenquist with David Dalton, p. 83.
5 Rosenquist with David Dalton, p. 103.

Many of the earliest works are indeed enigmatic, more about the act of seeing and perceiving rather than suggesting a strict narrative. While *Zone* was an experiment in abstracting recognizable imagery through shifts in scale, *In the Red* (1962) is a domestic mise en scène, a surreal snapshot of a family living in debt, "the average bourgeois family that is always broke."[6] A scarlet bowl of Campbell's tomato soup, a man's stockinged feet, a stuffed chair set against a floral wall, a Band-Aid: the quotidian concerns of a family just scraping by.

In *4 Young Revolutionaries* (1962), Rosenquist explained "The identities of the four young revolutionaries are concealed behind objects that represent their attributes—and the image is seen through glass cracked by bullet holes. The idea was that these are the radicals who get sacrificed in any revolution.... As they move out of their frames they fade from our short-term historical memory.... By obscuring the features of the faces in these paintings, I removed an essential part of the representational imagery: the face. If anything, I've always thought of myself as an abstract painter, and what could be more nonobjective than something you can't remember."[7]

Conversely, Marilyn Monroe is one of a handful of unforgettable celebrities Rosenquist depicted. (Others include politician John F. Kennedy and the actress Joan Crawford.) Rosenquist recounted to me that he felt Marilyn was a victim of the system, a beautiful captive in a gilded cage, and remembered seeing her tip over a stack of newspapers at a kiosk in Irvington, New York. He understood the power of imagery, of celebrity, he understood that even making her image into a patchwork of snippets—some upside down—people would still recognize her iconic visage. The immediacy and visual power of advertising was still at work when he DID abstract her image, as in *Marilyn Monroe I* (1962) currently in the collection of the Museum of Modern Art. With Marilyn Monroe—a face that had saturated the media for at least a decade before her death in August 1962—it was almost impossible to make her image unrecognizable.

Rosenquist painted *The Promenade of Merce Cunningham* (1963) to benefit the Foundation for the Contemporary Performance Arts, with the proceeds supporting grants to avant-garde performances of music, dance, and theater in New York. (Dancer and choreographer Merce Cunningham was slated to receive one such grant from the FCPA for a downtown performance.) The work is a brilliant and succinct pun, a pair of stiff leather shoes traipsing across a backdrop of pasta salad, interleafed with the face of a woman who is presumably the observer or audience of this action. The painting *Portrait of the Scull Family* (1962) may appear oblique, unless the viewer is aware Robert and Ethel Scull owned a taxicab fleet (a fact directly referenced in the open cab door and taxi fare lettering in the center of the painting). The source collage includes a photo of Ethel Scull, although her portrait didn't make it into the final composition. Robert and Ethel Scull were among Rosenquist's earliest collectors, and he was the financial backer of the groundbreaking Green Gallery (which gave Rosenquist his first solo exhibition in 1962). The Sculls purchased several of Rosenquist's early Pop paintings and were enthusiastic champions of the nascent Pop art movement.

Begun during an election year, the room-scale installation *Horse Blinders* (1968–69) was a political statement. "I decided to do a big painting where you couldn't see left, and you couldn't see right. You could only see straight ahead. *Horse Blinders* was the result. It was neither right wing nor left wing. In that sense, as in *F-111* (1964–65) [Rosenquist's first room-scale installation that addressed the Vietnam War], the painting was about peripheral

6 Rosenquist with David Dalton, p. 89.
7 Rosenquist with David Dalton, pp. 110-112.

vision, about looking at something and questioning it because of everything else you're seeing at the same time, the things on the peripheries that affect your vision." While the politics of the work, with its telephone cables and melting butter in a hot saucepan, may not be readily apparent, to Rosenquist "the telephone company was public enemy number one. There were ethical questions being discussed involving government spying.... we were concerned about the Vietnam War and the scandal of the Pentagon Papers." Rosenquist was never monolithic in his work. There are other stories rippling across the four walls: "You know, existence is like a piece of hot butter in a frying pan," as one of his studio assistants once said. According to Rosenquist, "life is like a quick burn, a quick sizzle. It's an existential idea."[8] The painting was exhibited at Leo Castelli Gallery—installed in the front room (as *F-111* had been in 1965). It was promptly purchased by the German collector Dr. Peter Ludwig during the installation (before the show opened) and now resides in the collection of the Museum Ludwig in Cologne, Germany, which has one of the largest collections of Pop art outside of the United States.

When we were installing Rosenquist's retrospective at the Guggenheim Museum in New York in 2003, the artist walked into the rotunda to see the progress. The early works from the 1960s, including *Zone* and *President Elect*, were being installed on the lower ramps that day. Rosenquist looked up the spiral ramps almost dazed, bewildered in a positive way. I asked how he was feeling, and he said it was like seeing all his children again after years and years apart. An emotional reunion. The effect was spectacular: the ability to see the artworks spiral up the ramps in 360-degree fashion, a dialogue not only between works hung next to each other and in adjacent bays, but across the ramps and in the round. Not every show works well on the Guggenheim's ramps—each exhibition is an intervention in the Frank Lloyd Wright circular architecture—but Rosenquist's work was a perfect marriage with the building. The smaller paintings fit well in the lower bays, which gradually grow in height as one ascends to the upper ramps (just as Rosenquist's paintings grew taller and larger as the decades rolled on), and the tower galleries—rectangular galleries that shoot off the ramps on various floors—housed his largest paintings and room-scale explorations. The collages were also featured in large groupings in the rectangular tower galleries. The surrealist impulse, the plays with abstraction using recognizable imagery, the existential questions parsed with humor and puns: decades of his work pinged around the museum in a fashion that the late critic Peter Schjeldahl called "a pinball machine" in a review of the 2003 retrospective. In the early 1960s, Rosenquist went from billboard artist to American artist, adapting our national character and consumer interests into artworks of mystery and intrigue. He frequently told me the hardest thing to find as an artist is an idea, and that the best works ask questions rather than offer answers. His works continue to implore, intrigue, and captivate anew.

> *Popular culture isn't a freeze frame; it is images zapping by in rapid-fire succession, which is why collage is such an effective way of representing contemporary life. The blur between images creates a kind of motion of the mind.* James Rosenquist [9]

Sarah C. Bancroft
Head Curator, Estate of James Rosenquist

8 All quotes in this paragraph are from James Rosenquist with David Dalton, pp. 196 and 198 respectively.
9 James Rosenquist with David Dalton, p. 101.

ZONE

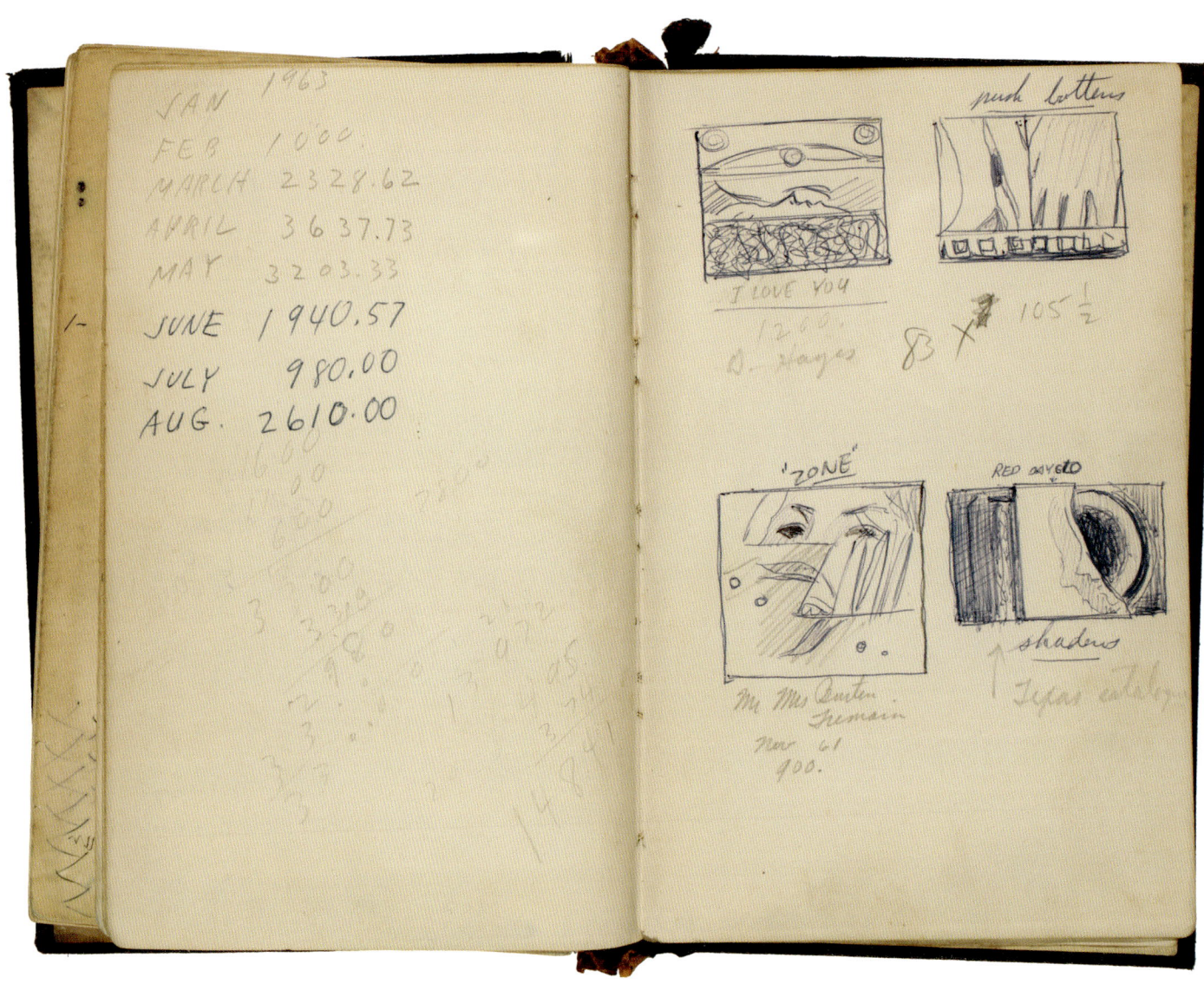

Ink and pencil sketch for *Zone* [lower left image on recto]
From "Coenties Slip Sketchbook," ca. 1960–63
Graphite, ink, crayon, and colored pencil on paper (hardcover sketchbook)
8 1/2" x 5 1/2" (21.6 x 14.0 cm) [closed]; 8 1/2" x 11 1/2" (21.6 x 29.2 cm) [opened overall]
Collection of the Estate of James Rosenquist

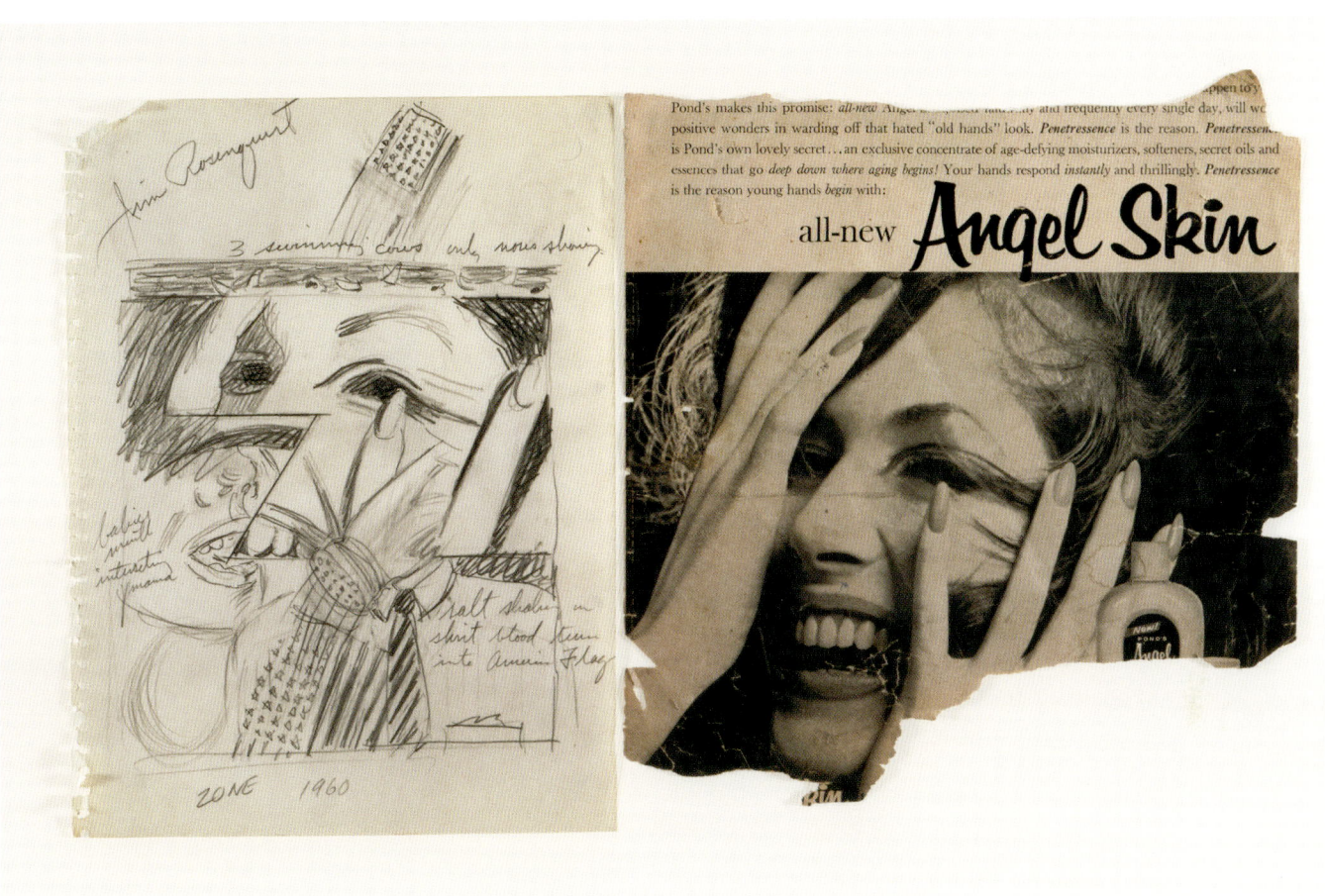

Preliminary Study and Source for *Zone*, 1960
Graphite on paper and magazine advertisement cutout; mounted on paper
11¹/₈" x 18⁵/₈" (28.3 x 47.3 cm)
Collection of the Estate of James Rosenquist

Zone, 1960–61
Oil on canvas
95" x 95 1/2" (241.3 x 242.6 cm)
Philadelphia Museum of Art, Purchased with the Edith H. Bell Fund, 1982 [1982-9-1]

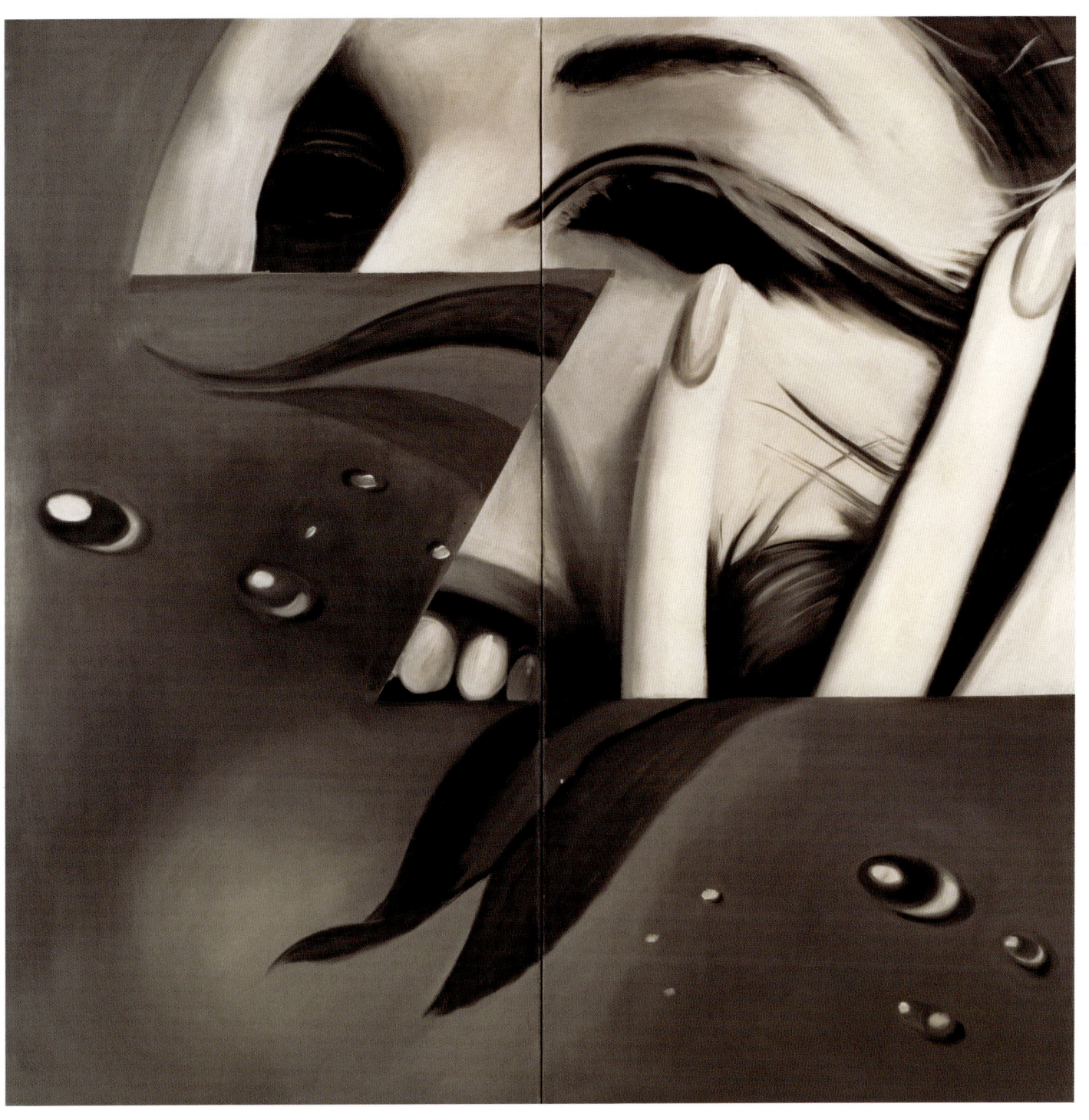

I Love You with My Ford

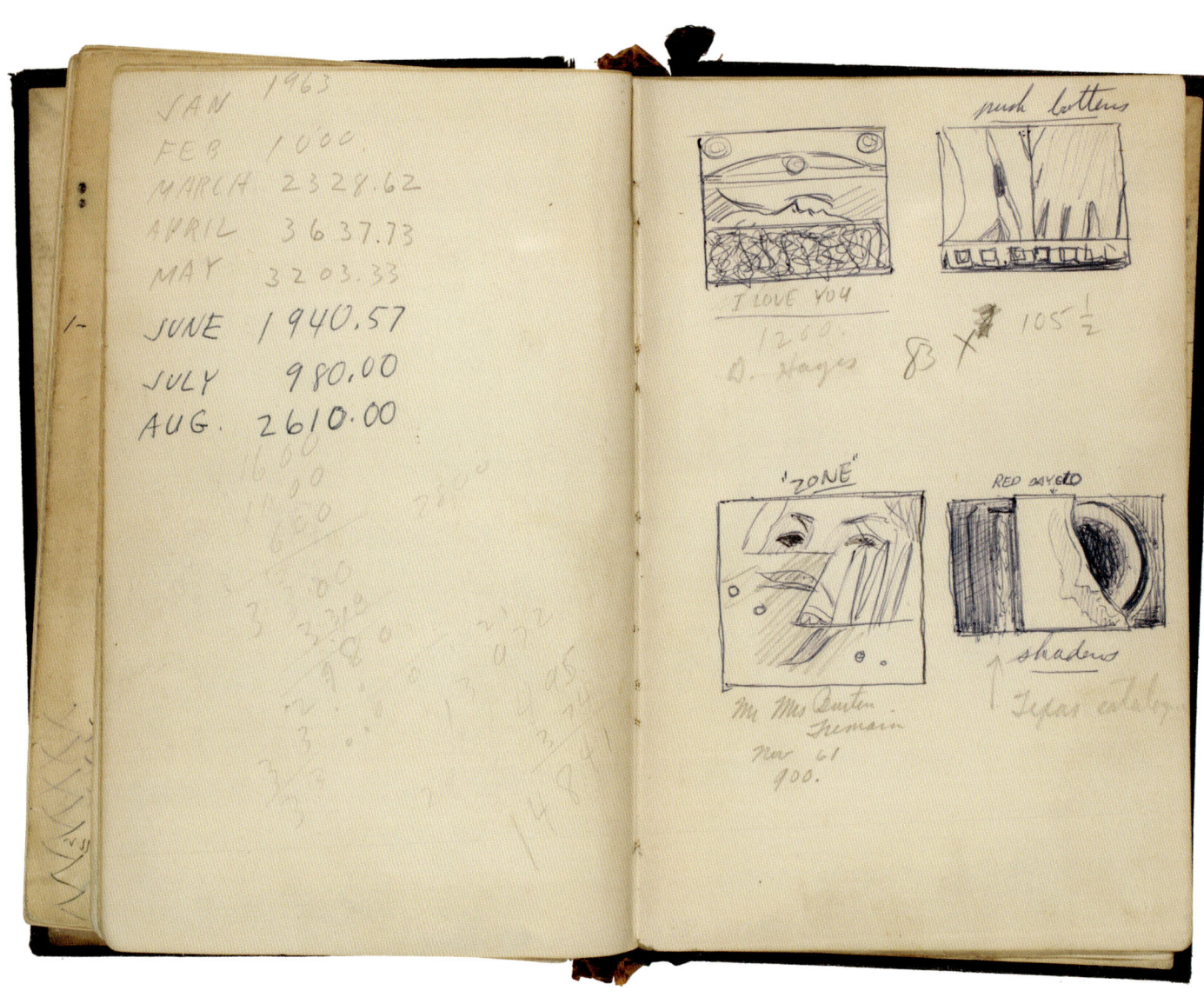

Ink sketch for *I Love You with My Ford* [upper left image on recto]
From "Coenties Slip Sketchbook," ca. 1960–63
Graphite, ink, crayon, and colored pencil on paper (hardcover sketchbook)
8 1/2" x 5 1/2" (21.6 x 14 cm) [closed]; 8 1/2" x 11 1/2" (21.6 x 29.2 cm) [opened overall]
Collection of the Estate of James Rosenquist

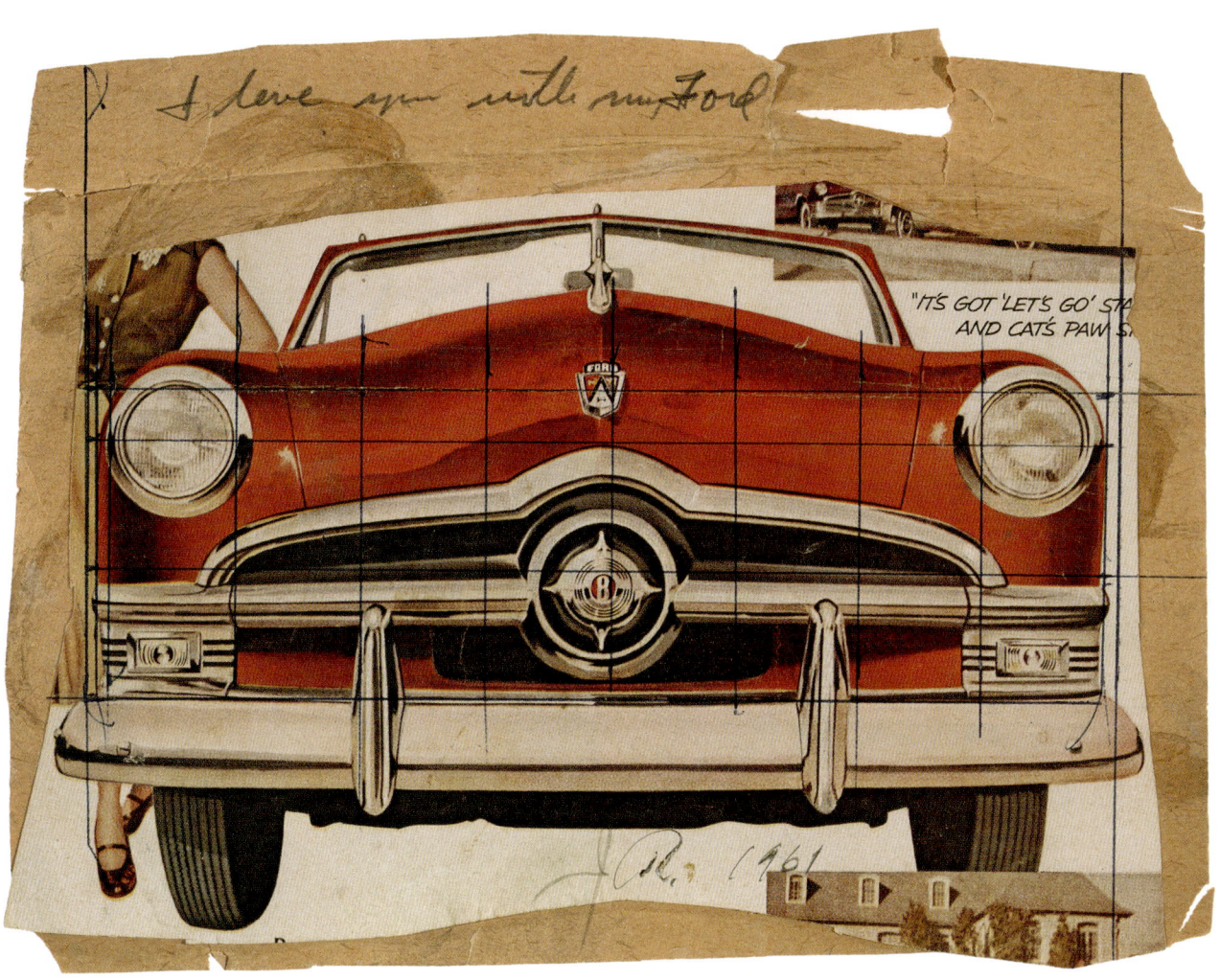

Source for *I Love You with My Ford*, 1961
Collage (magazine advertisement cutout) and ink on paper
7¼" x 9¹³/₁₆" (18.4 x 24.9 cm)
Collection of the Estate of James Rosenquist

I Love You with My Ford, 1961
Oil on canvas
82 3/4" x 93 1/2" (210.2 x 237.5 cm)
Moderna Museet, Stockholm [NM 5813]

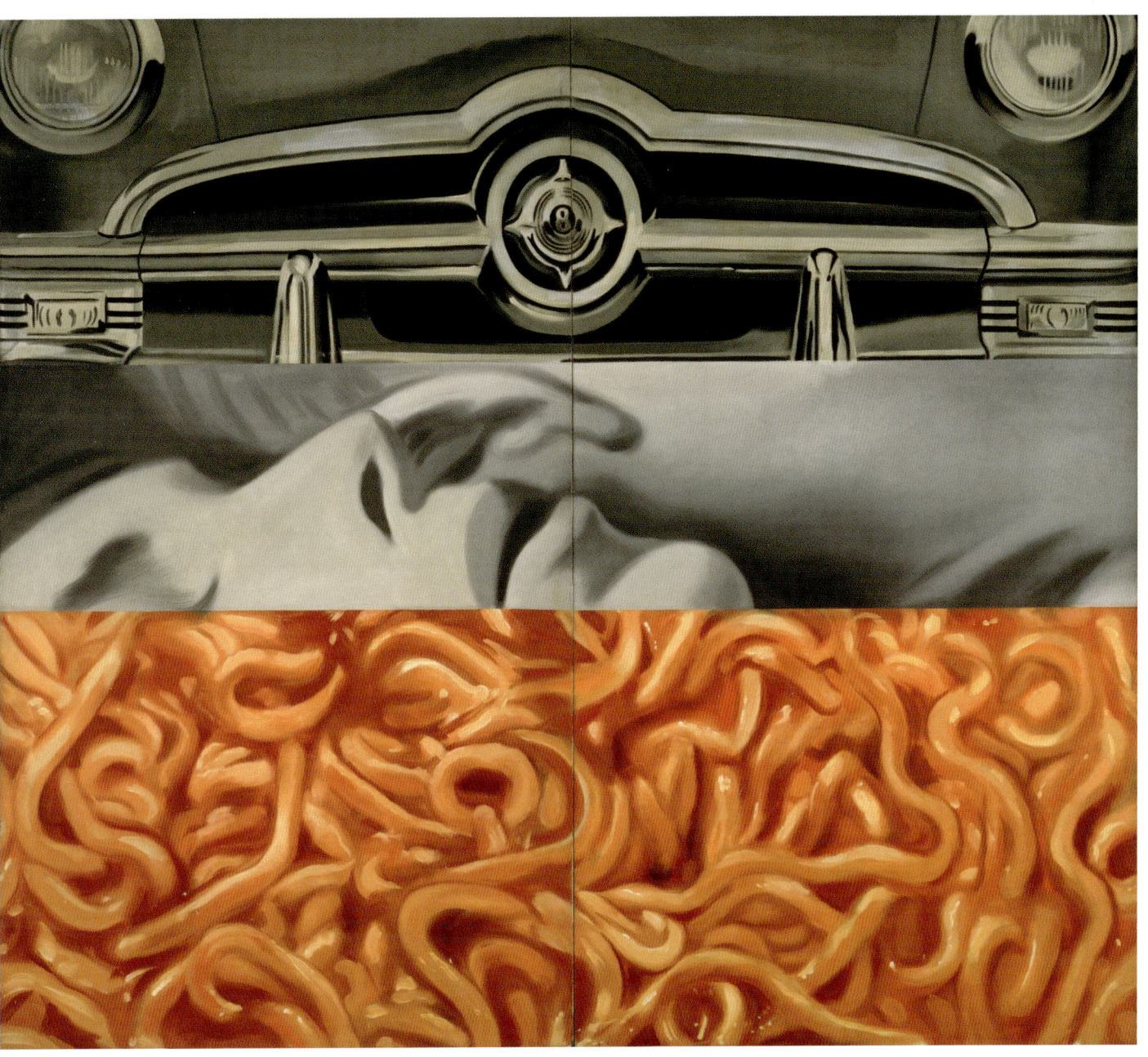

Marilyn Monroe I

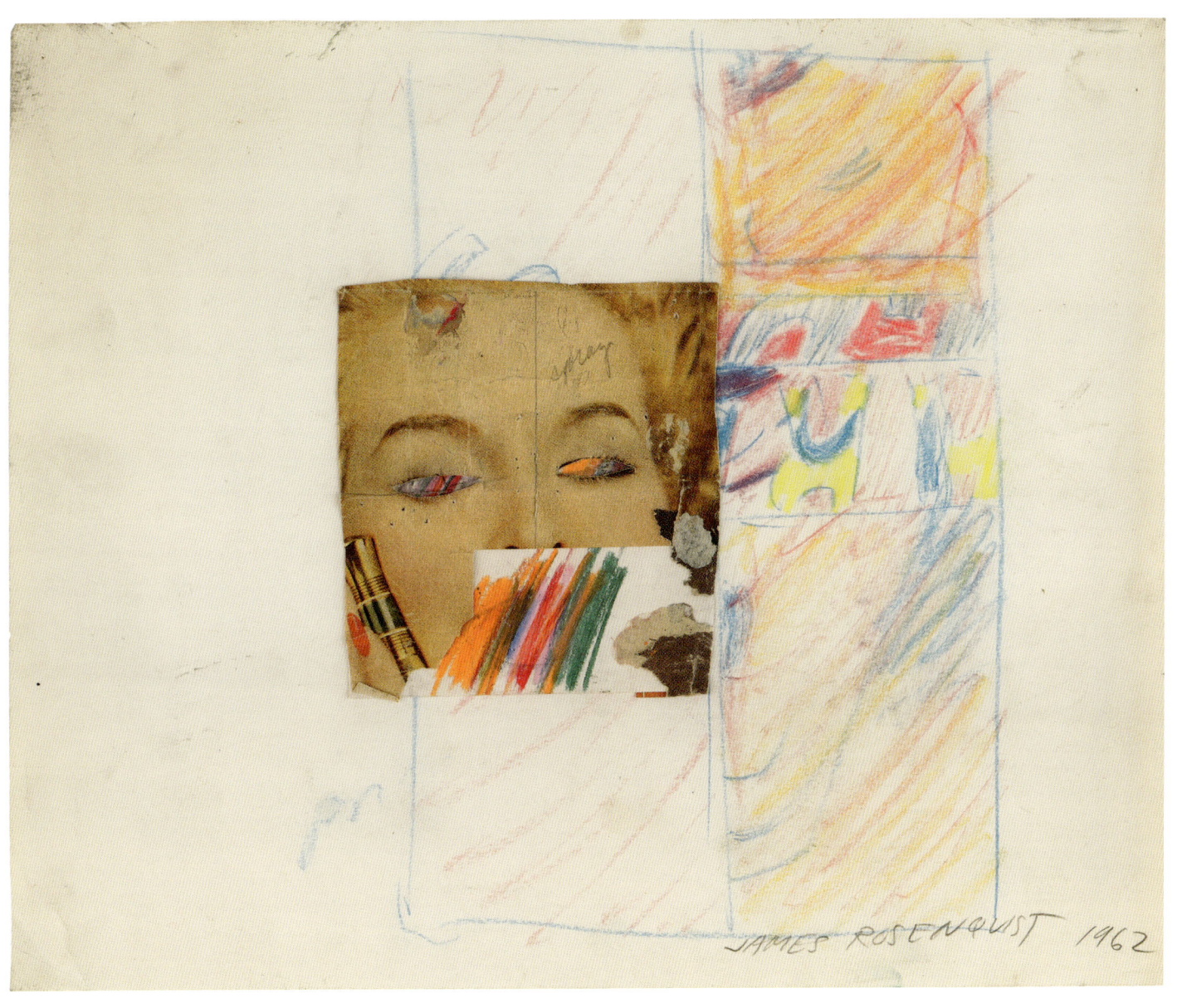

Study for Marilyn Monroe, 1962
Collage (magazine advertisement cutout) and colored pencil on paper
11¼" x 13¾" (28.6 x 34.9 cm)
Jack Shear Collection

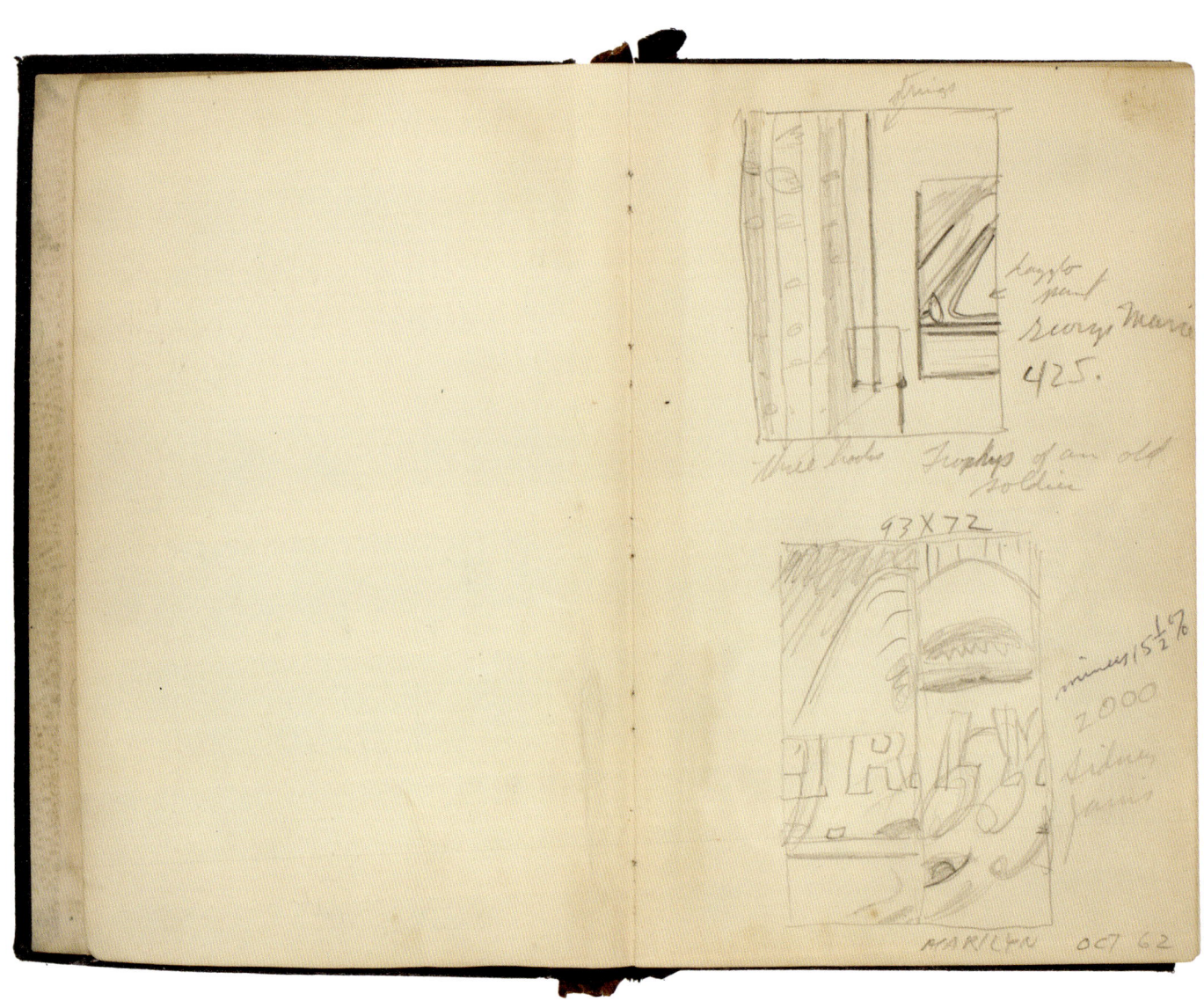

Pencil sketch for *Marilyn Monroe I* [lower image on recto]
From "Coenties Slip Sketchbook," ca. 1960–63
Graphite, ink, crayon, and colored pencil on paper (hardcover sketchbook)
8 1/2" x 5 1/2" (21.6 x 14.0 cm) [closed]; 8 1/2" x 11 1/2" (21.6 x 29.2 cm) [opened overall]
Collection of the Estate of James Rosenquist

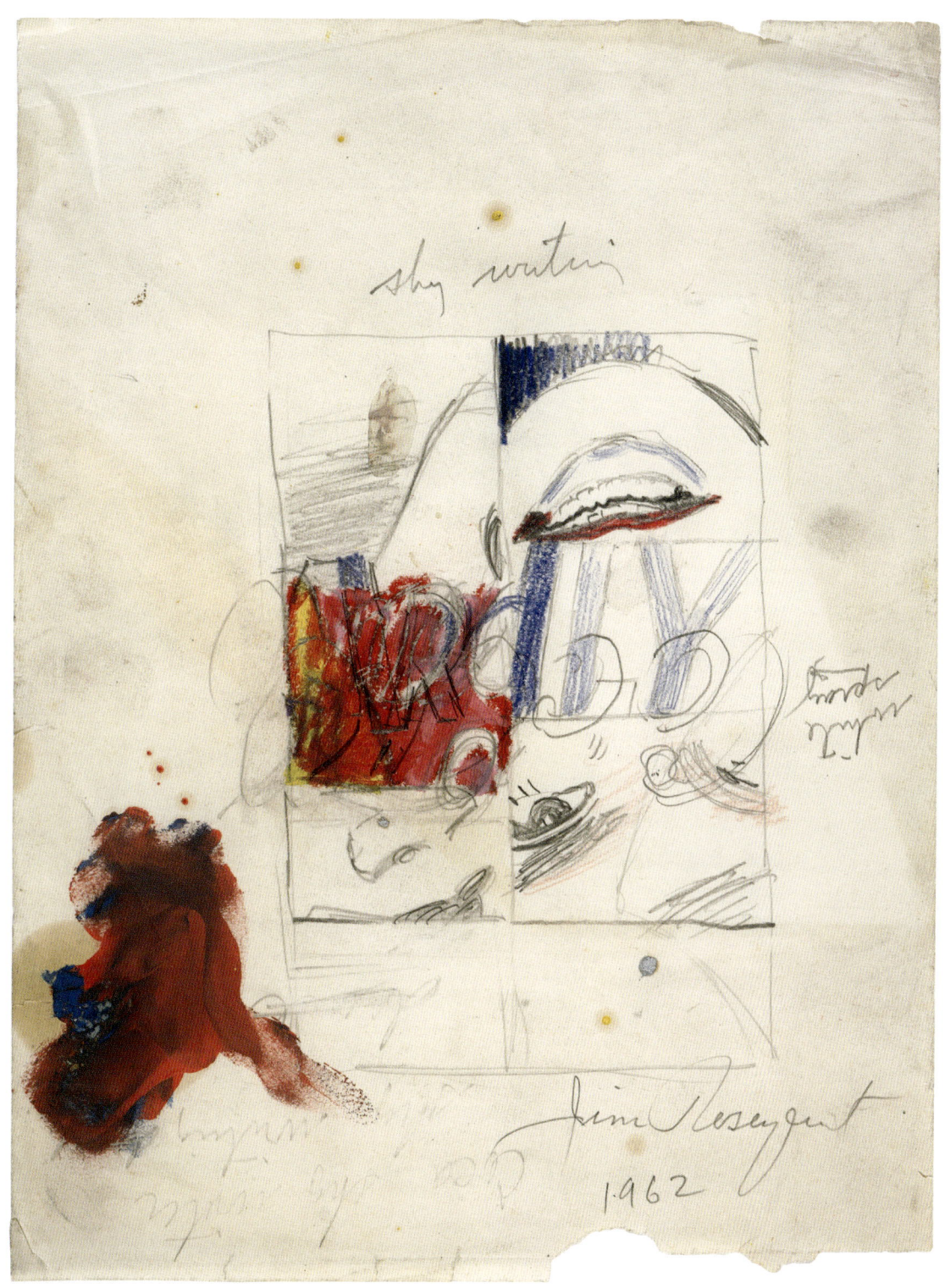

Sketch for Marilyn Monroe I, 1962
Graphite, crayon, and paint, with adventitious marks, on paper
11 15/16" x 8 15/16" (30.3 x 22.7 cm)
Private Collection

Marilyn Monroe I, 1962
Oil and spray enamel on canvas
93" x 72¼" (236.2 x 183.5 cm)
The Museum of Modern Art, New York, The Sidney and Harriet Janis Collection [646.67]

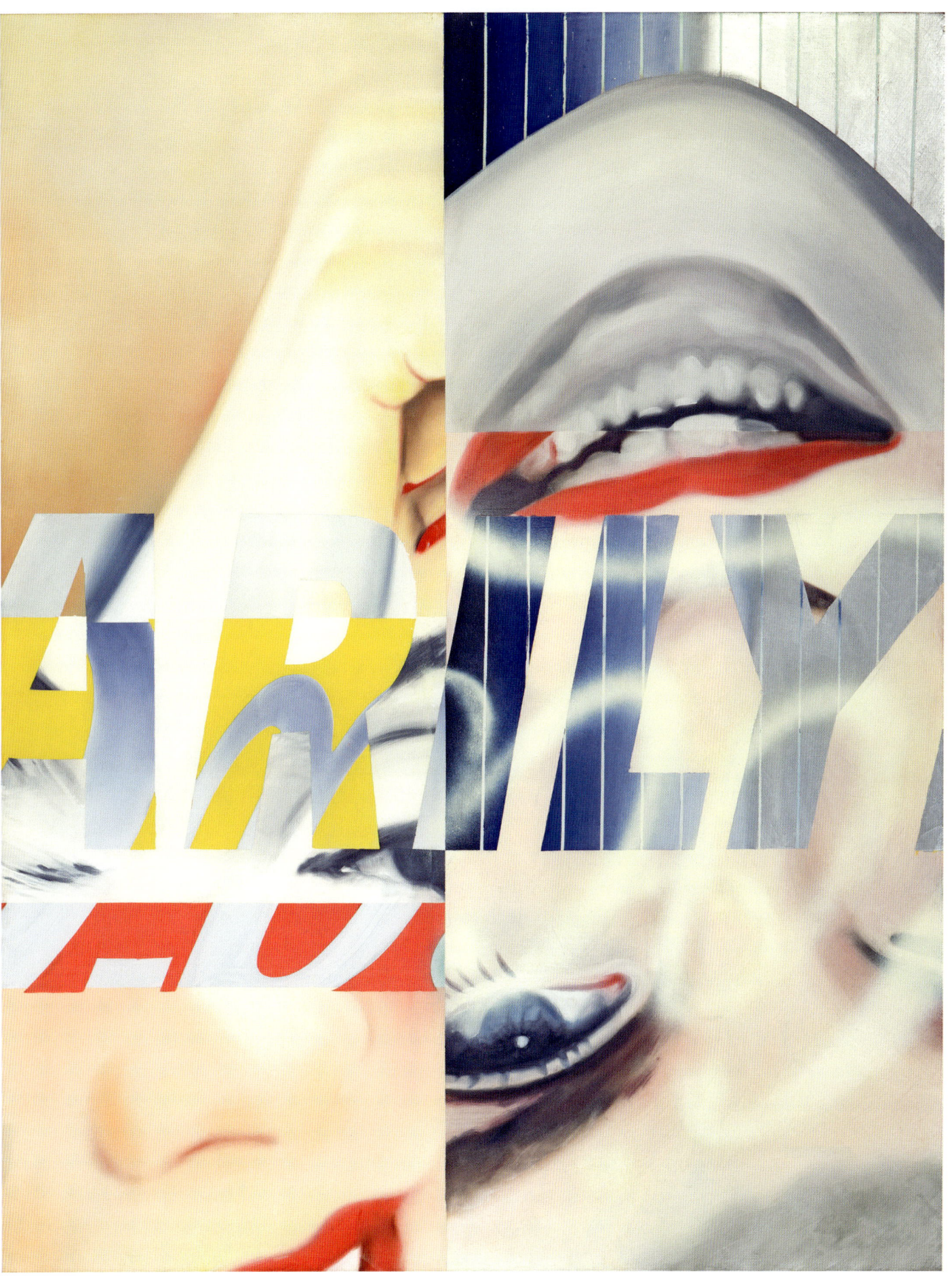

Study for Marilyn

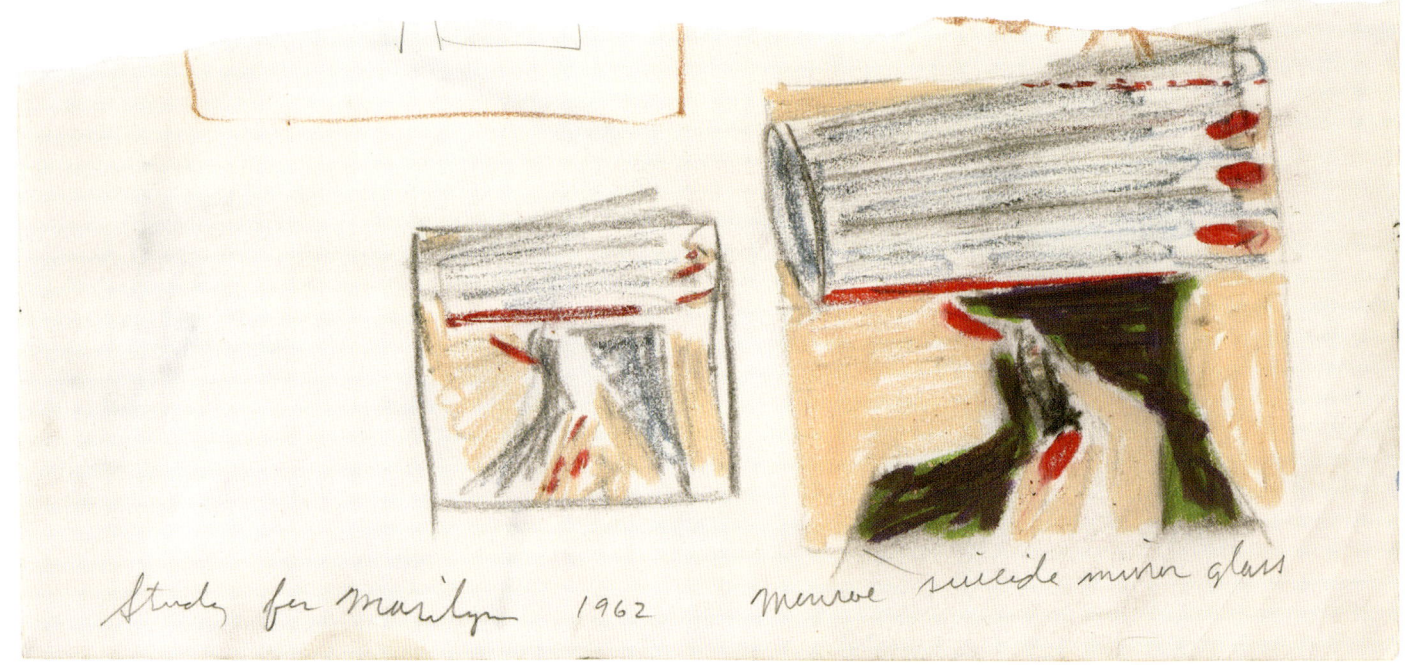

Study for Marilyn, 1962
Crayon and graphite on paper
6 ^{9}/$_{16}$" x 14 ^{1}/$_{16}$" (16.7 x 35.7 cm)
Collection of the Estate of James Rosenquist

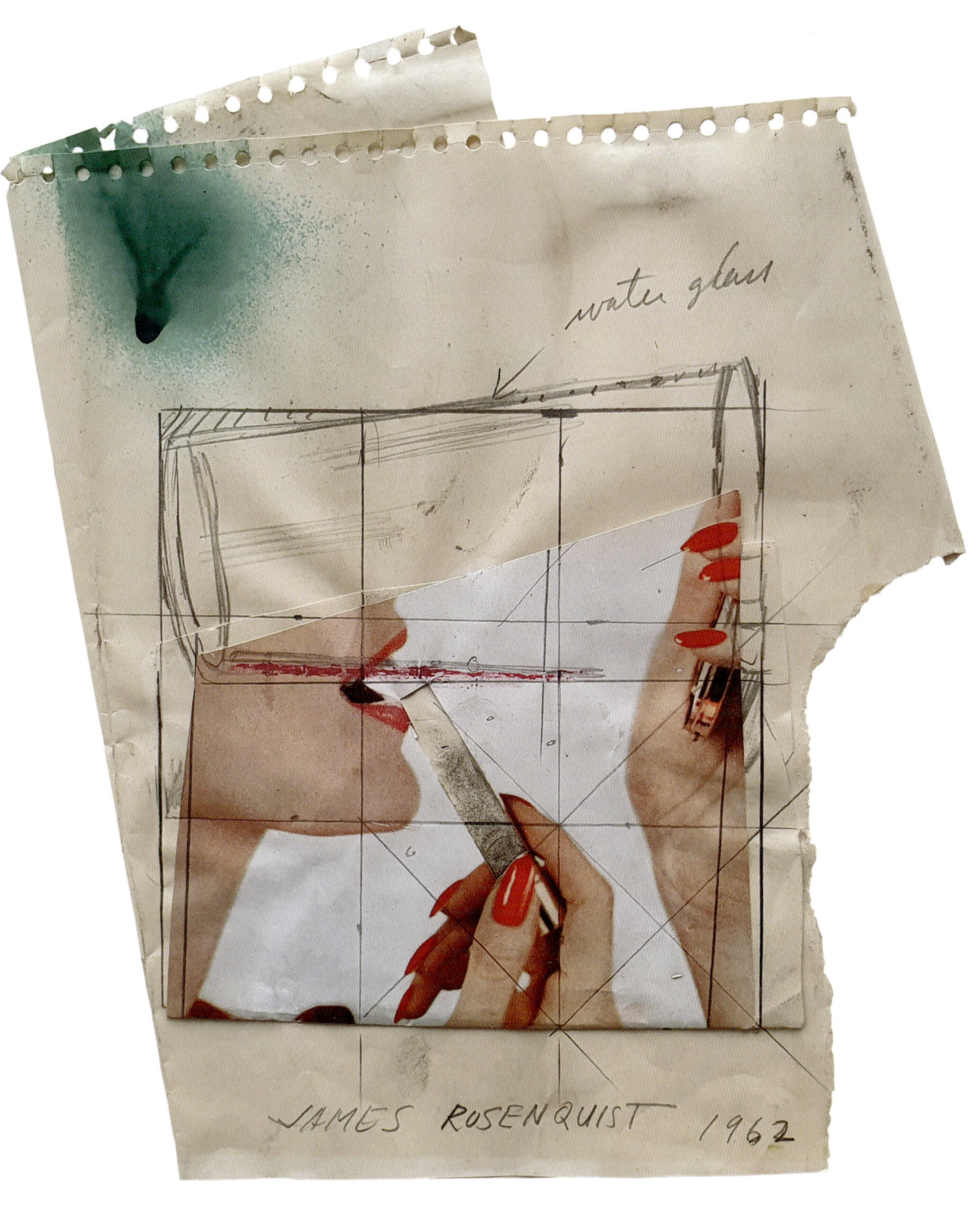

Source for *Study for Marilyn*, 1962
Collage (magazine advertisement cutout) and mixed media on paper
11" x 9¹⁄₁₆" (27.9 x 23.0 cm) [approx.]
Private Collection

Study for Marilyn, 1962
Oil on canvas and shaped hardboard
38" x 36" (96.5 x 91.4 cm)
Private Collection

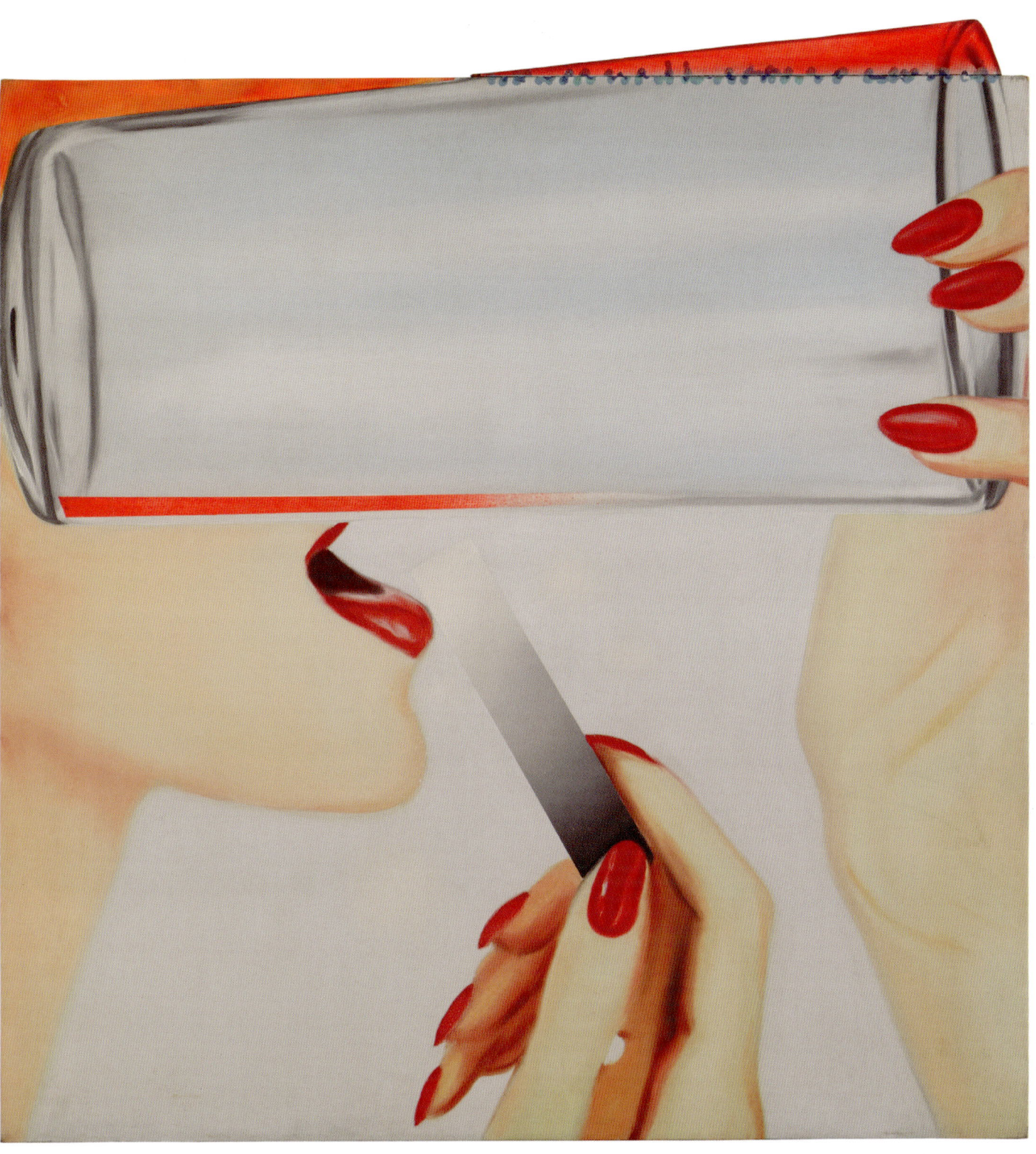

In the Red

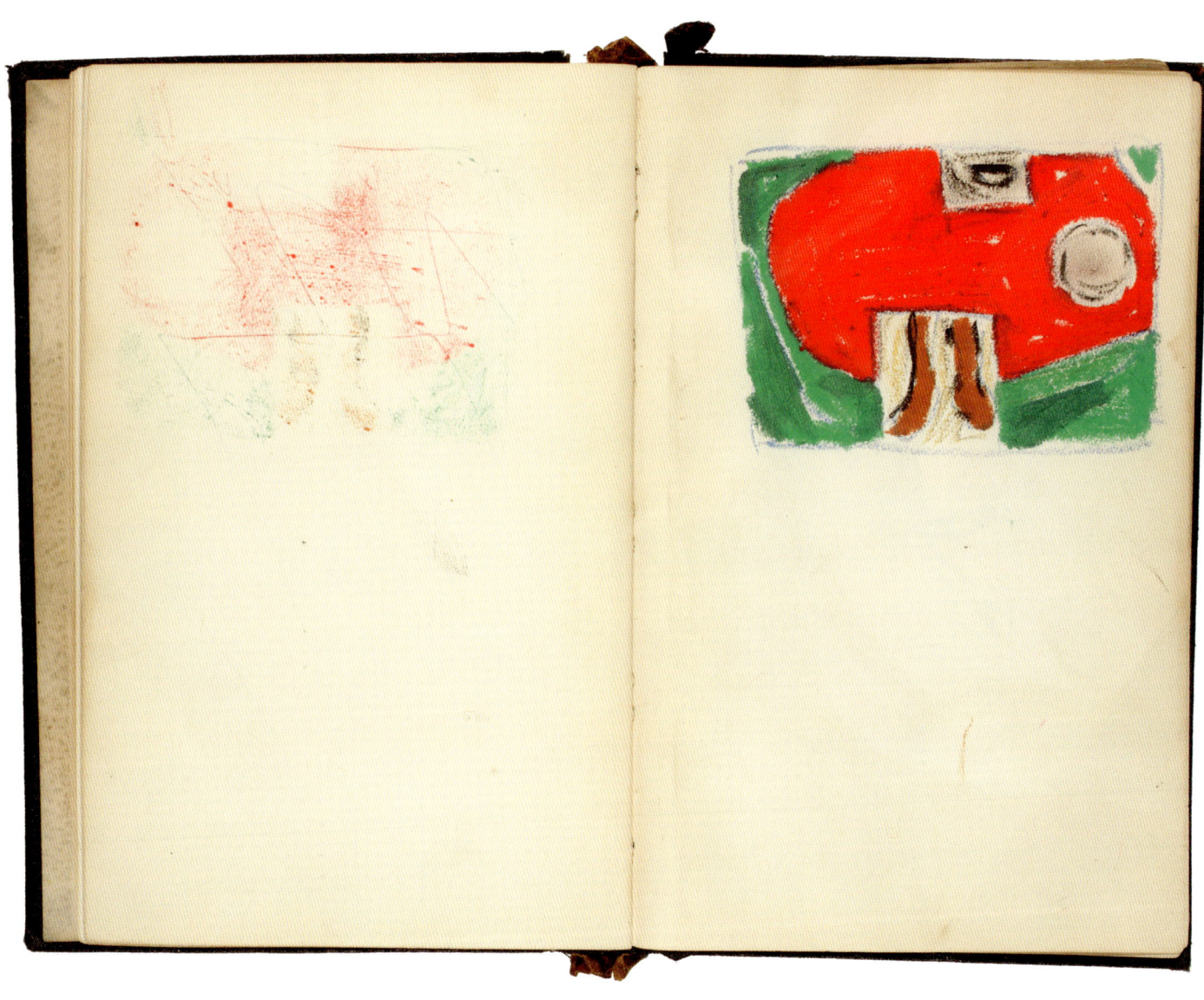

Crayon sketch for *In the Red* [image on recto]
From "Coenties Slip Sketchbook," ca. 1960–63
Graphite, ink, crayon, and colored pencil on paper (hardcover sketchbook)
8 1/2" x 5 1/2" (21.6 x 14.0 cm) [closed]; 8 1/2" x 11 1/2" (21.6 x 29.2 cm) [opened overall]
Collection of the Estate of James Rosenquist

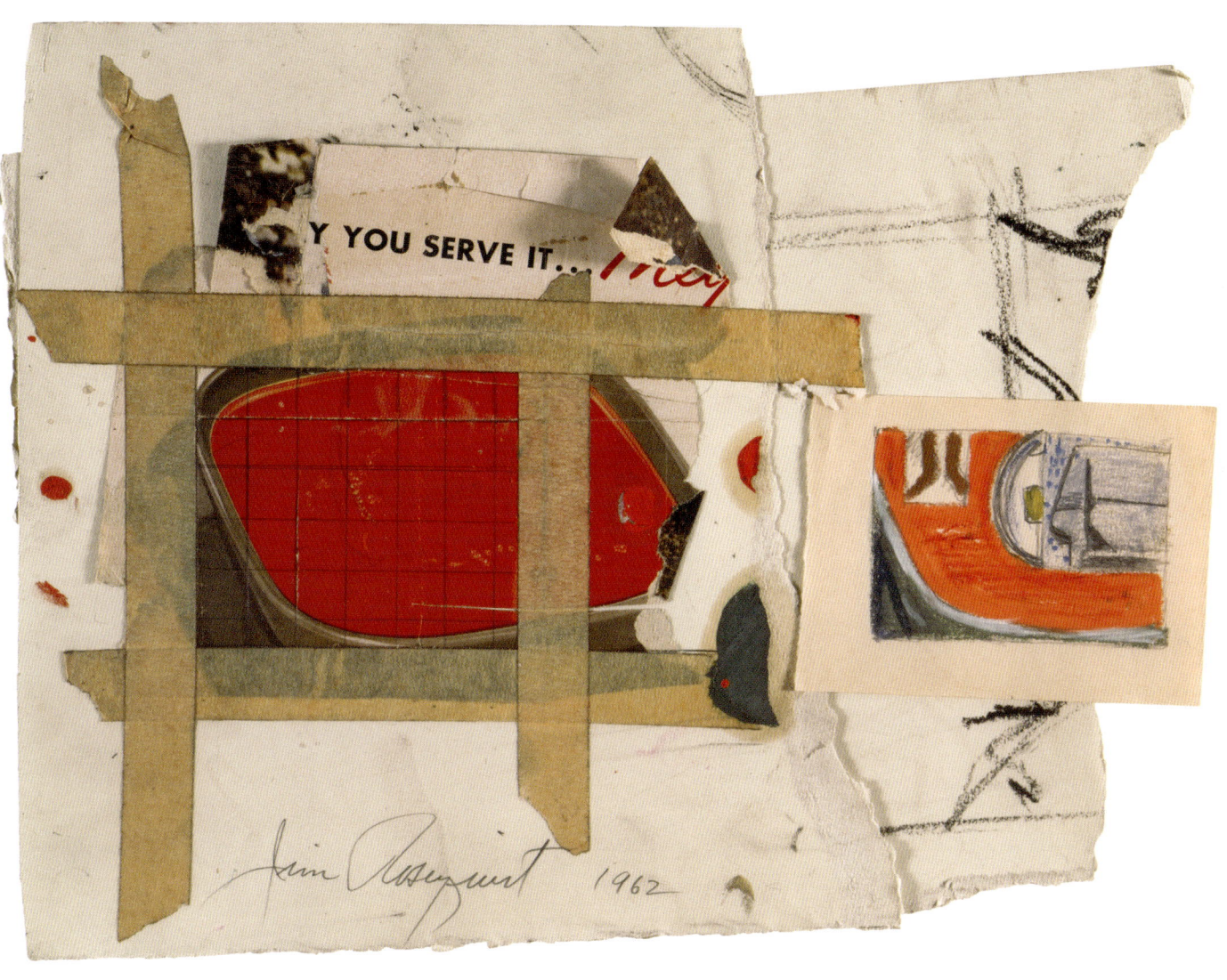

Source and Preparatory Study for *In the Red*, 1962
Collage (magazine advertisement cutout, paper) and mixed media
(graphite, crayon, paint, masking tape), with adventitious marks, on paper
9¼" x 12⁷⁄₁₆" (23.5 x 31.6 cm)
Collection of the Estate of James Rosenquist

In the Red, 1962
Oil on canvas
66 1/4" x 78 1/4" (168.3 x 198.8 cm)
Private Collection

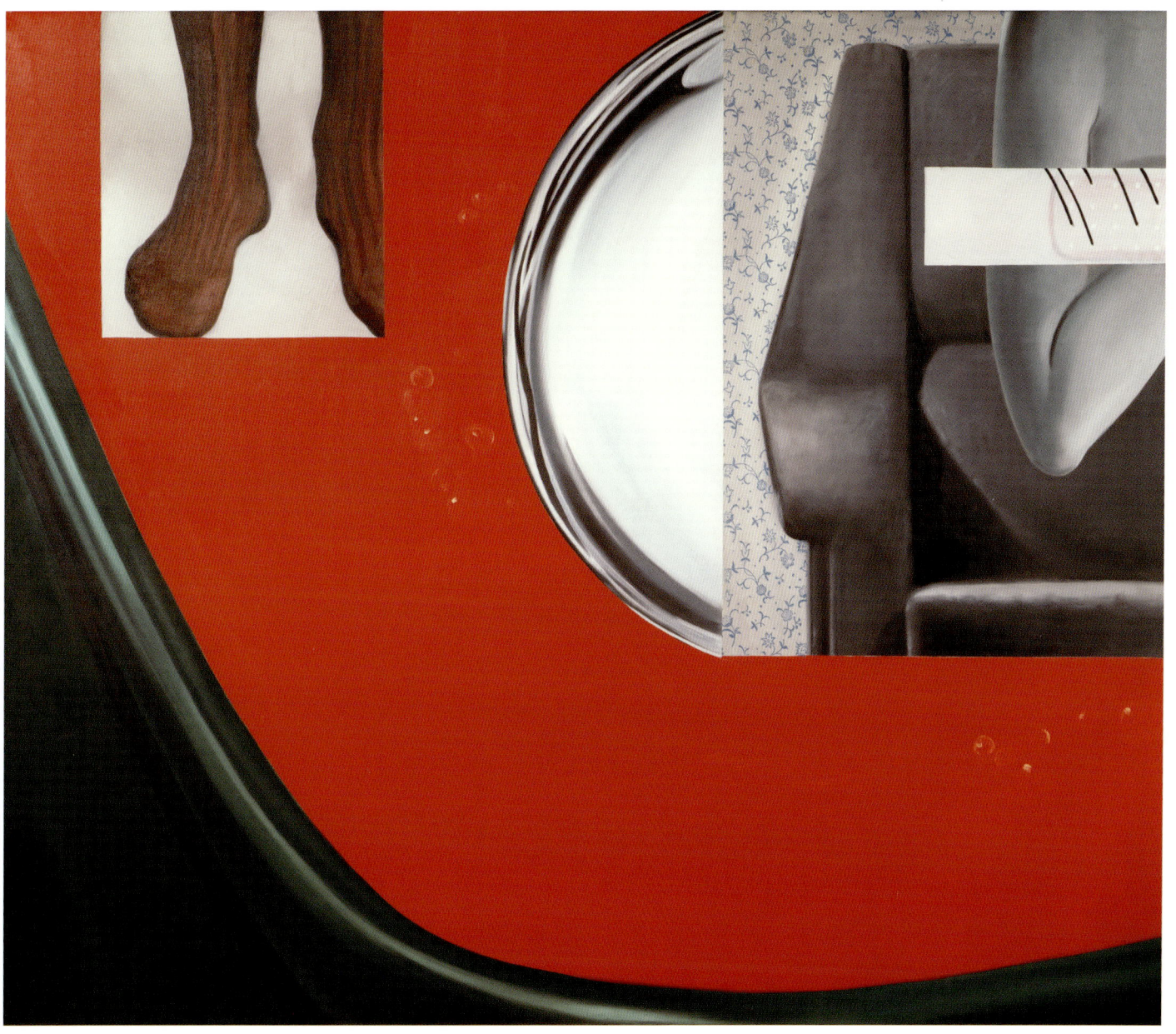

4 Young Revolutionaries

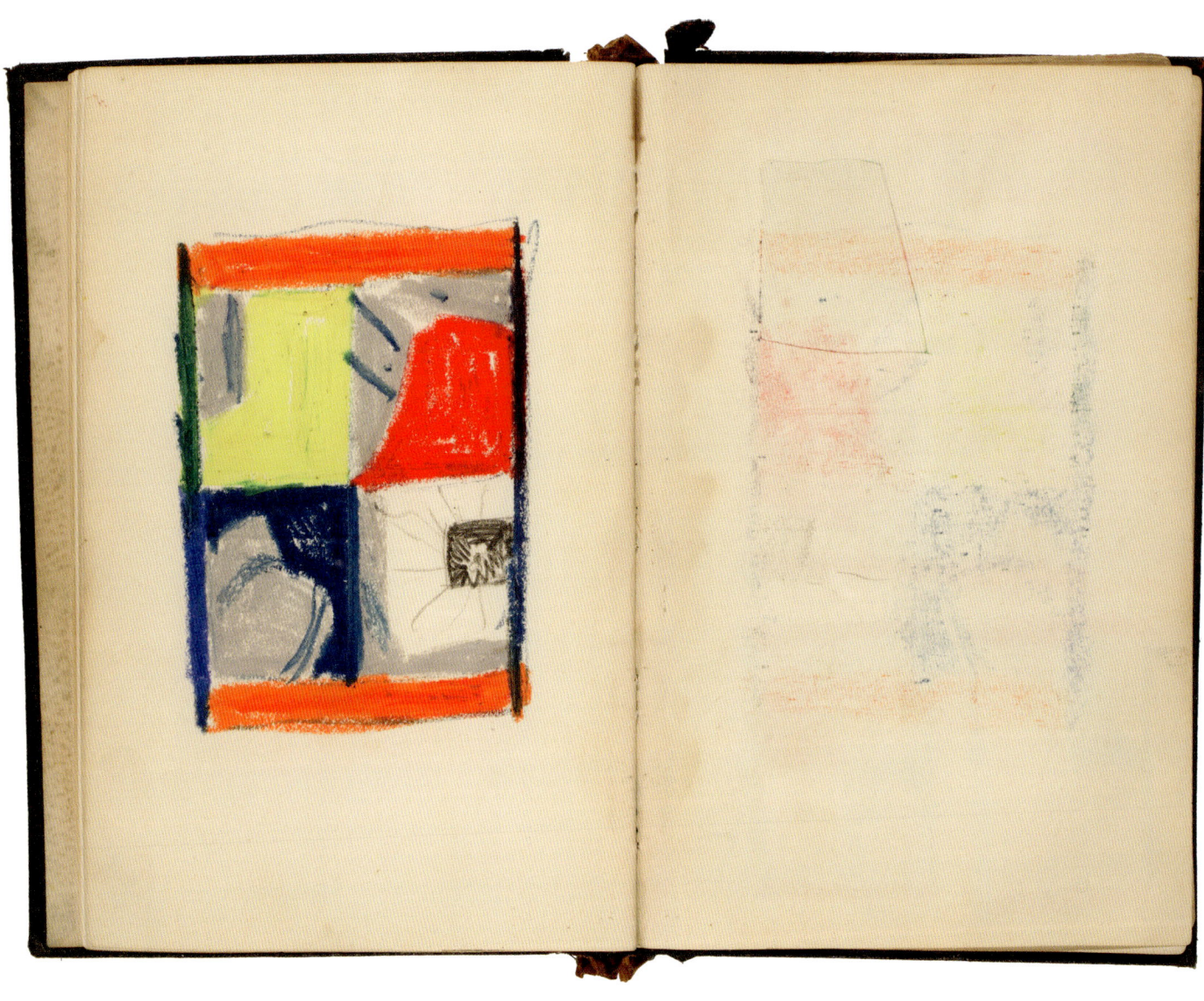

Crayon sketch for *4 Young Revolutionaries* [image on verso]
From "Coenties Slip Sketchbook," ca. 1960–63
Graphite, ink, crayon, and colored pencil on paper (hardcover sketchbook)
8 1/2" x 5 1/2" (21.6 x 14.0 cm) [closed]; 8 1/2" x 11 1/2" (21.6 x 29.2 cm) [opened overall]
Collection of the Estate of James Rosenquist

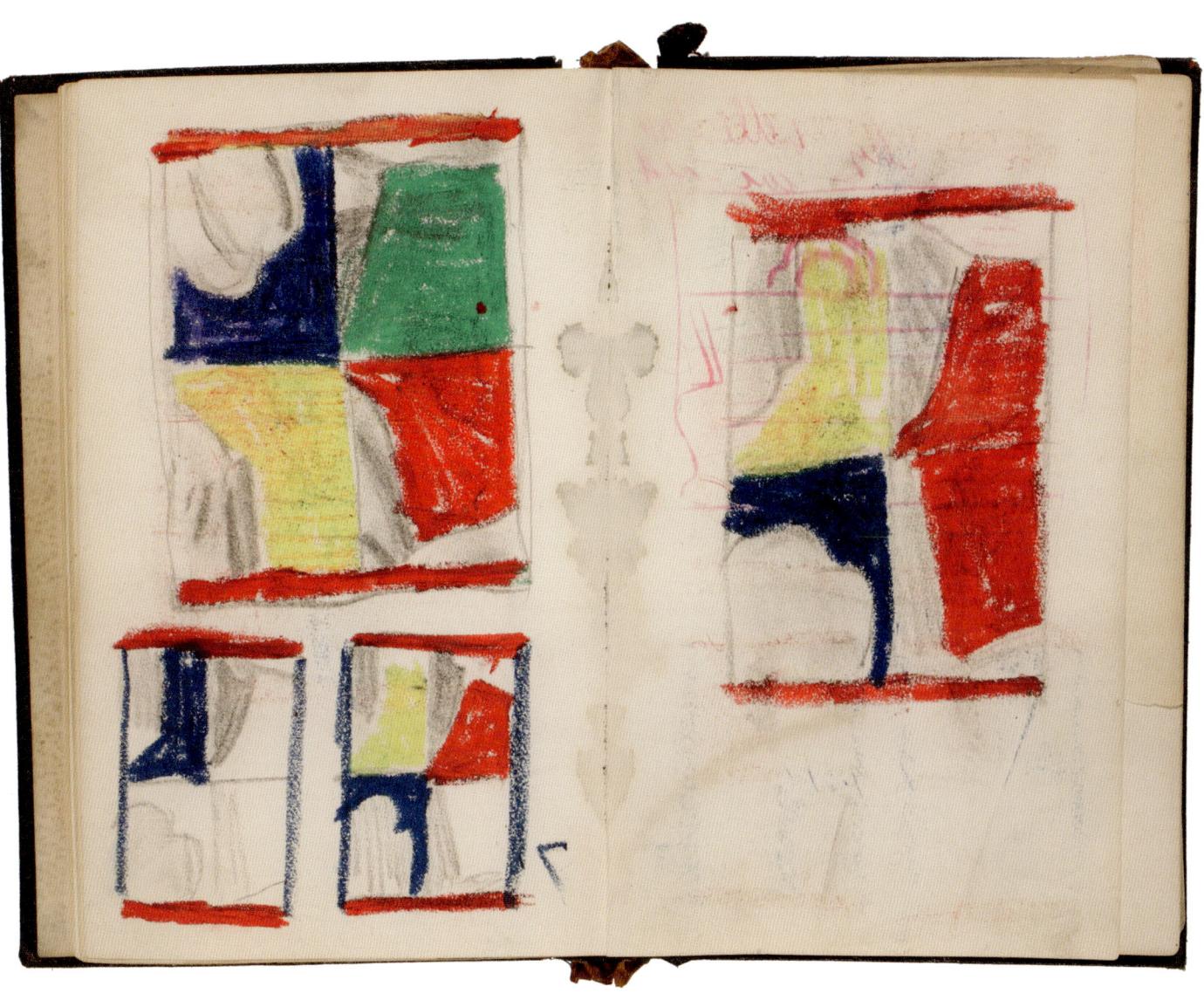

Crayon sketches for *4 Young Revolutionaries* [images on verso and recto]
From "Coenties Slip Sketchbook," ca. 1960–63
Graphite, ink, crayon, and colored pencil on paper (hardcover sketchbook)
8 ¹/₂" x 5 ¹/₂" (21.6 x 14.0 cm) [closed]; 8 ¹/₂" x 11 ¹/₂" (21.6 x 29.2 cm) [opened overall]
Collection of the Estate of James Rosenquist

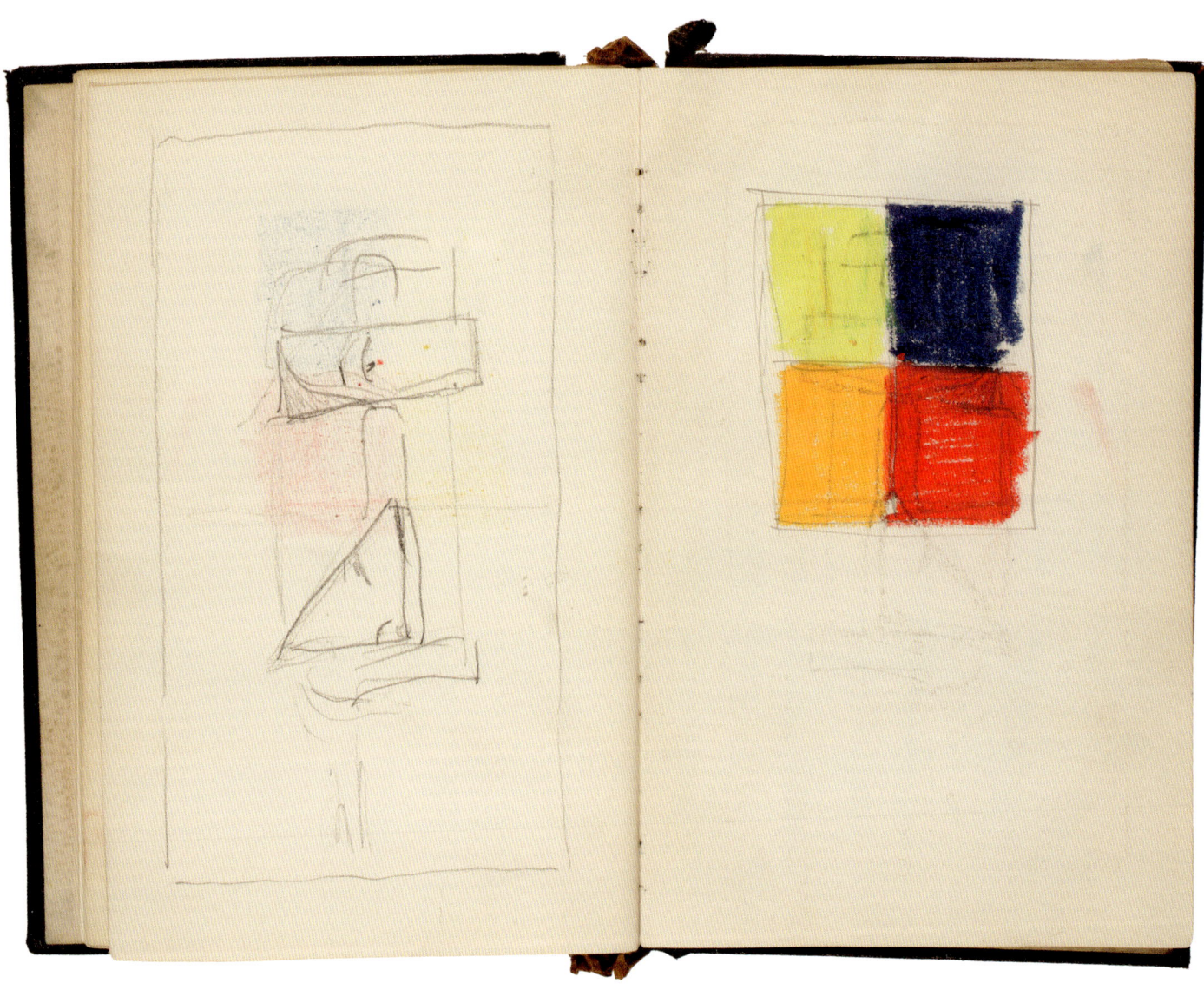

Crayon sketch for *4 Young Revolutionaries* [image on recto]
From "Coenties Slip Sketchbook," ca. 1960–63
Graphite, ink, crayon, and colored pencil on paper (hardcover sketchbook)
8 1/2" x 5 1/2" (21.6 x 14.0 cm) [closed]; 8 1/2" x 11 1/2" (21.6 x 29.2 cm) [opened overall]
Collection of the Estate of James Rosenquist

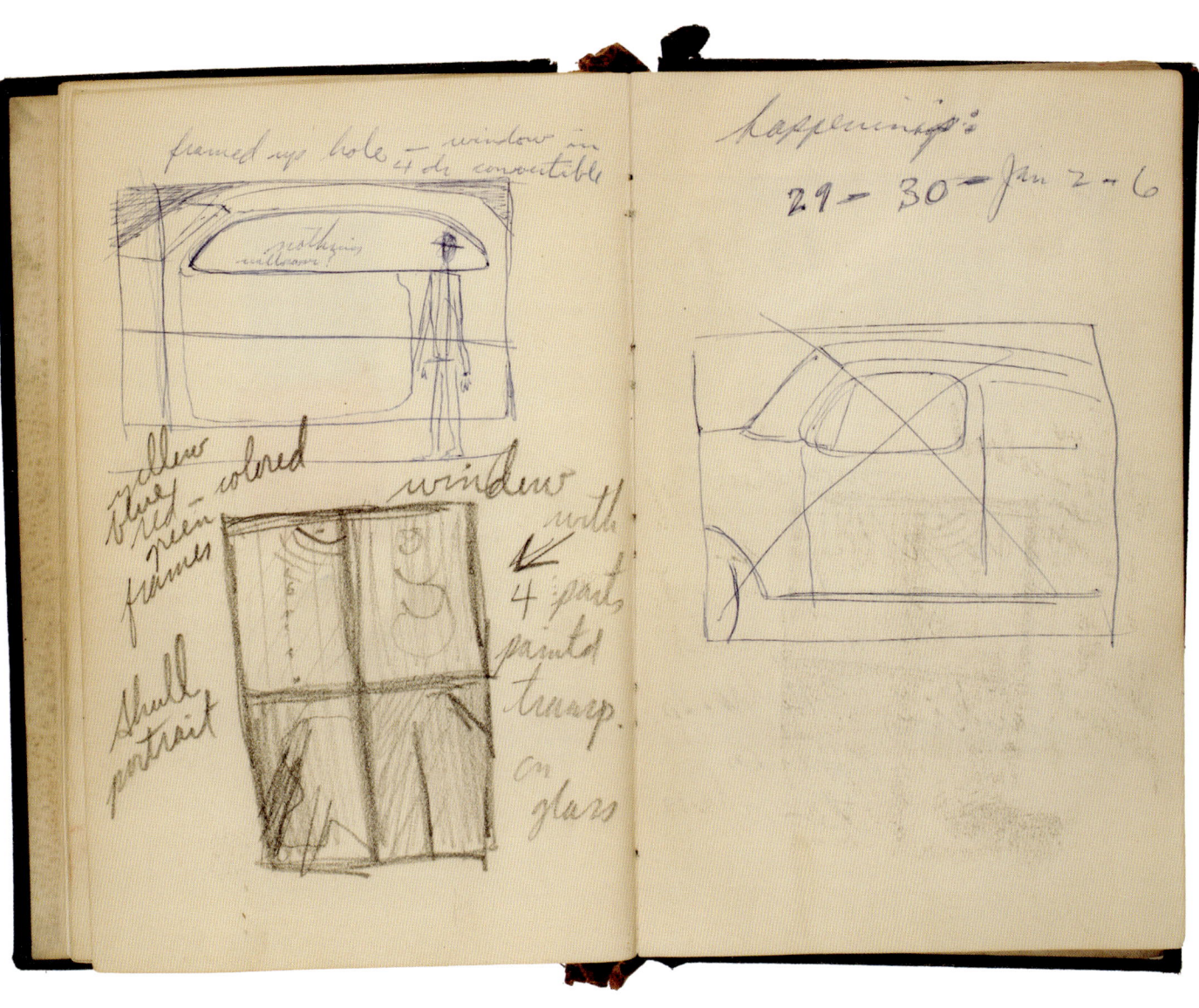

Pencil sketch for *4 Young Revolutionaries* [lower image on verso]
From "Coenties Slip Sketchbook," ca. 1960–63
Graphite, ink, crayon, and colored pencil on paper (hardcover sketchbook)
8 1/2" x 5 1/2" (21.6 x 14.0 cm) [closed]; 8 1/2" x 11 1/2" (21.6 x 29.2 cm) [opened overall]
Collection of the Estate of James Rosenquist

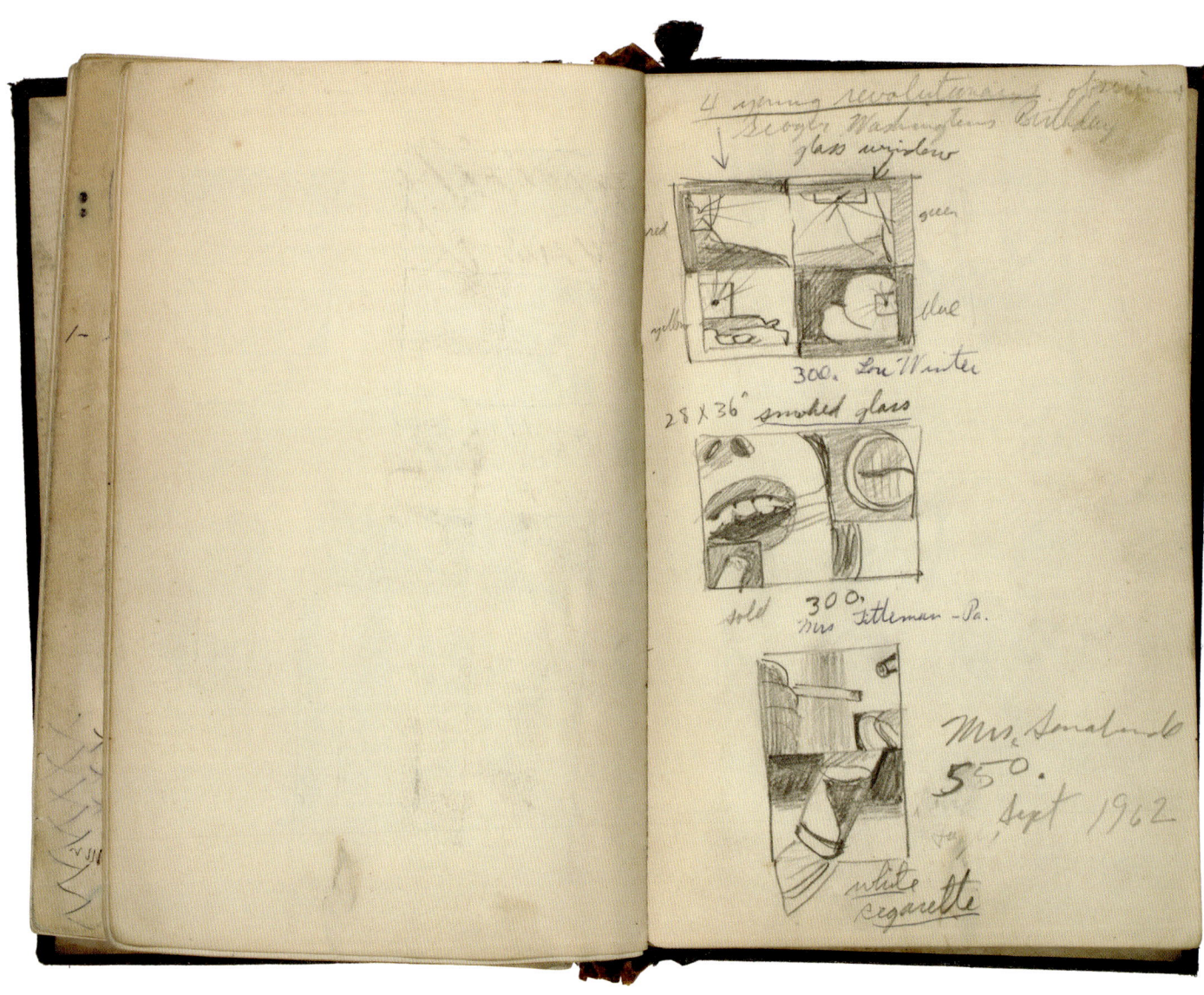

Pencil sketch for *4 Young Revolutionaries* [upper image on recto]
From "Coenties Slip Sketchbook," ca. 1960–63
Graphite, ink, crayon, and colored pencil on paper (hardcover sketchbook)
8 1/2" x 5 1/2" (21.6 x 14.0 cm) [closed]; 8 1/2" x 11 1/2" (21.6 x 29.2 cm) [opened overall]
Collection of the Estate of James Rosenquist

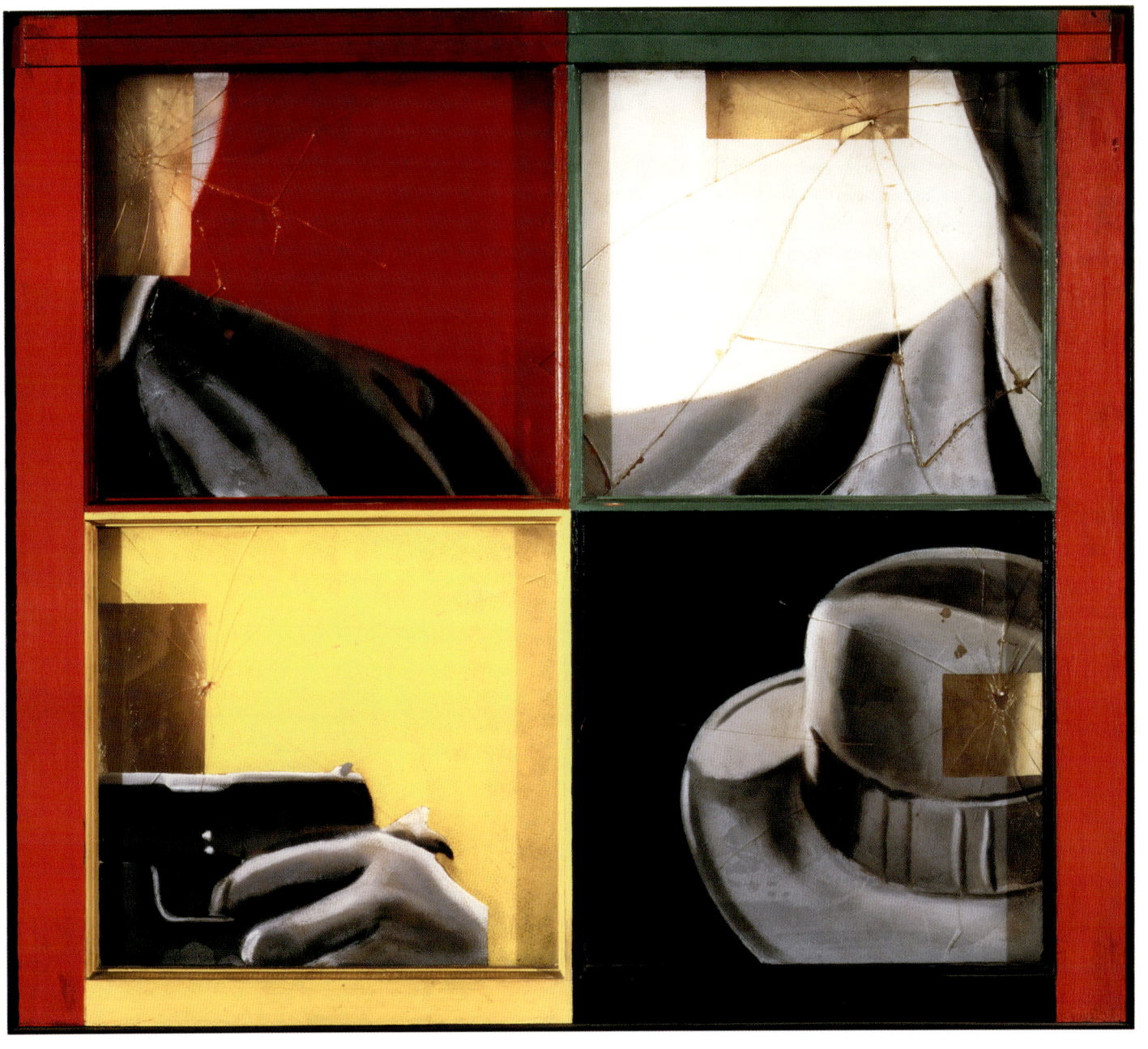

4 Young Revolutionaries, 1962
Oil on wood and glass
24" x 32" (61.0 x 81.3 cm)
Private Collection

A Lot to Like

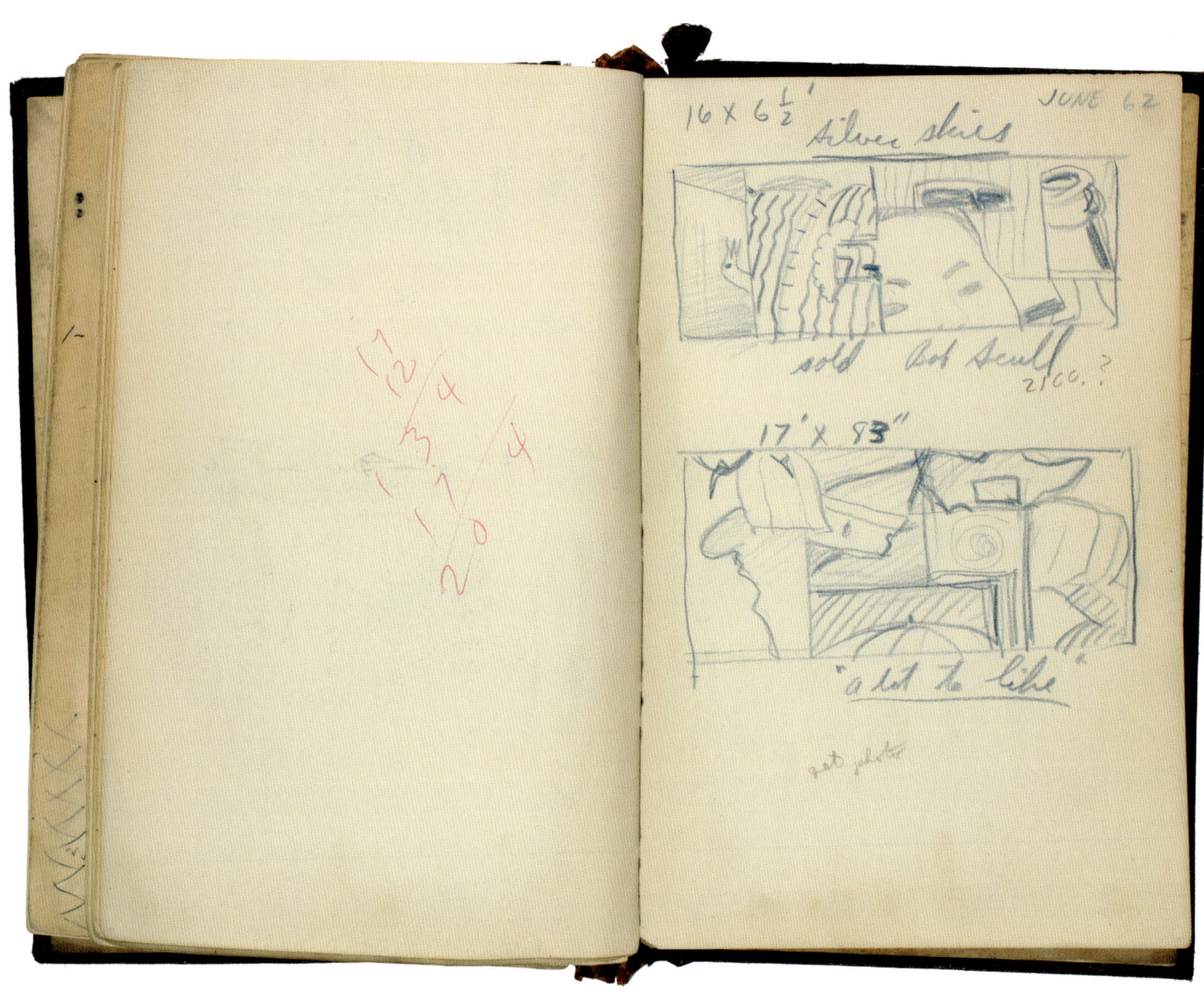

Colored pencil sketch for *A Lot to Like* [lower image on recto]
From "Coenties Slip Sketchbook," ca. 1960–63
Graphite, ink, crayon, and colored pencil on paper (hardcover sketchbook)
8 1/2" x 5 1/2" (21.6 x 14.0 cm) [closed]; 8 1/2" x 11 1/2" (21.6 x 29.2 cm) [opened overall]
Collection of the Estate of James Rosenquist

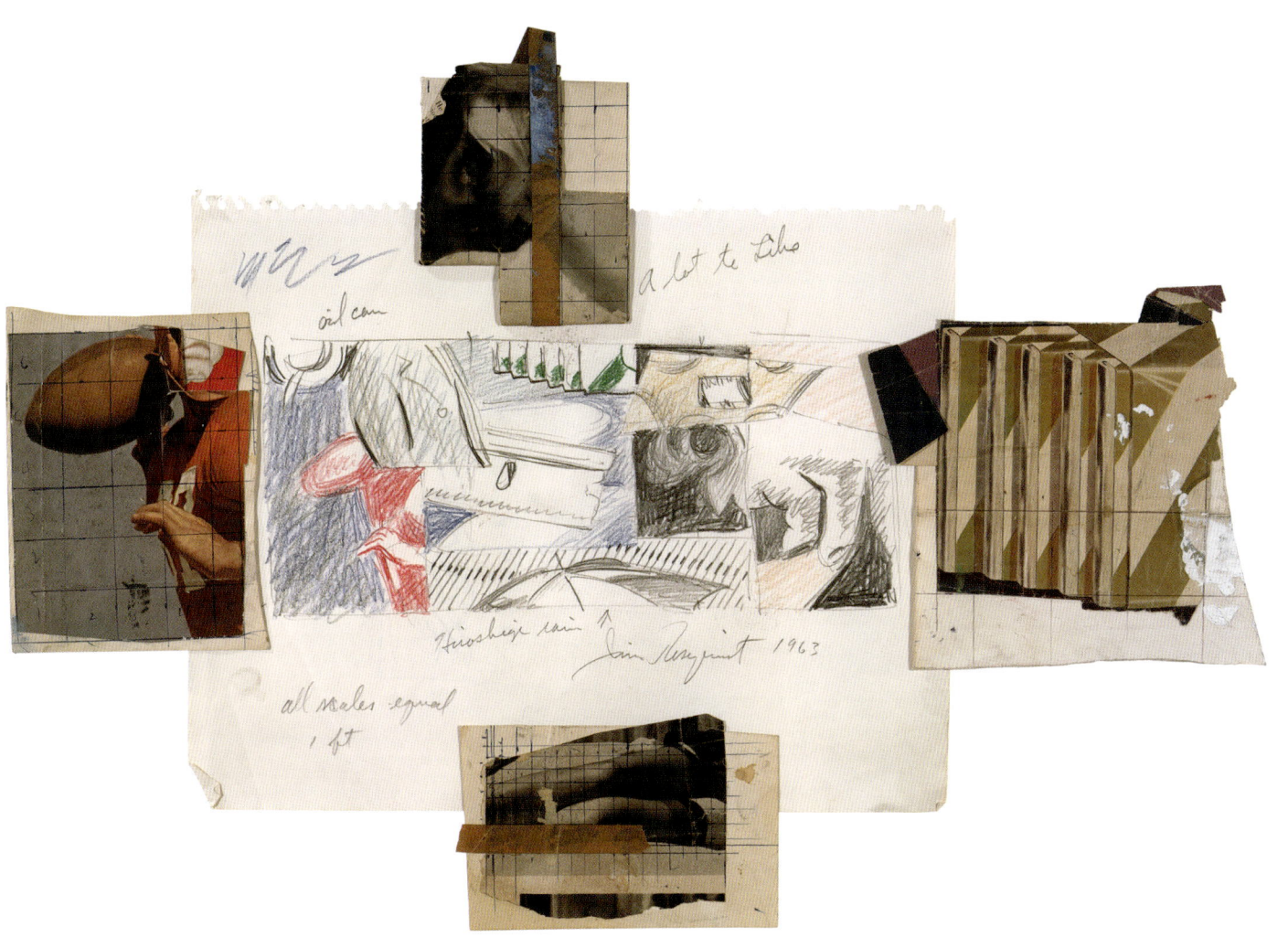

Sources and Preparatory Study for *A Lot to Like*, 1963
Collage (magazine advertisement cutouts) and mixed media
(ink, masking tape, graphite, crayon, paper, paint), with adventitious marks, on paper
16 1/16" x 23 1/8" (40.8 x 58.7 cm)
Collection of the Estate of James Rosenquist

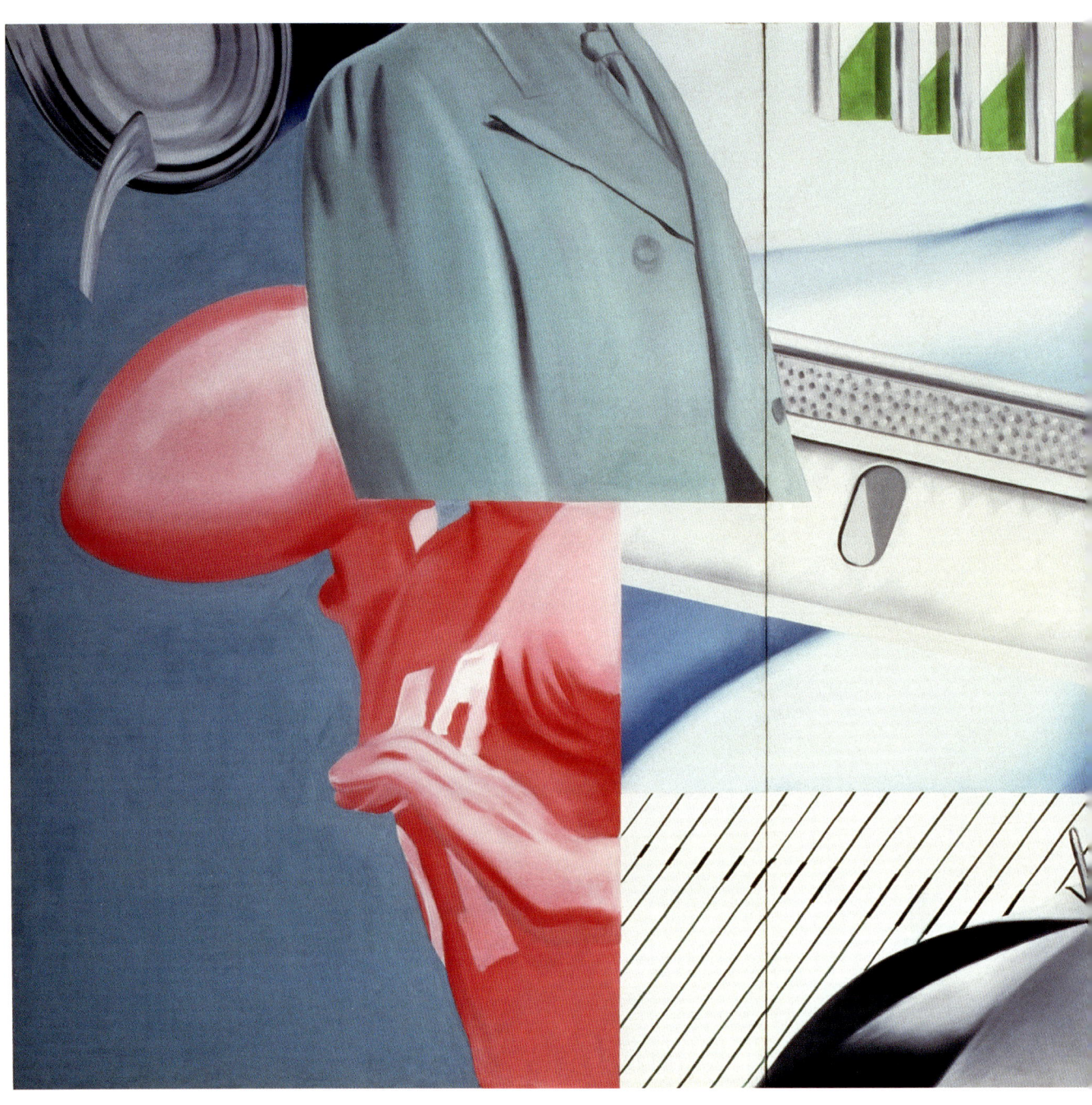

A Lot to Like, 1962
Oil on canvas
7' 9" x 17' (236.2 x 518.2 cm)
The Museum of Contemporary Art, Los Angeles, The Panza Collection [84.8]

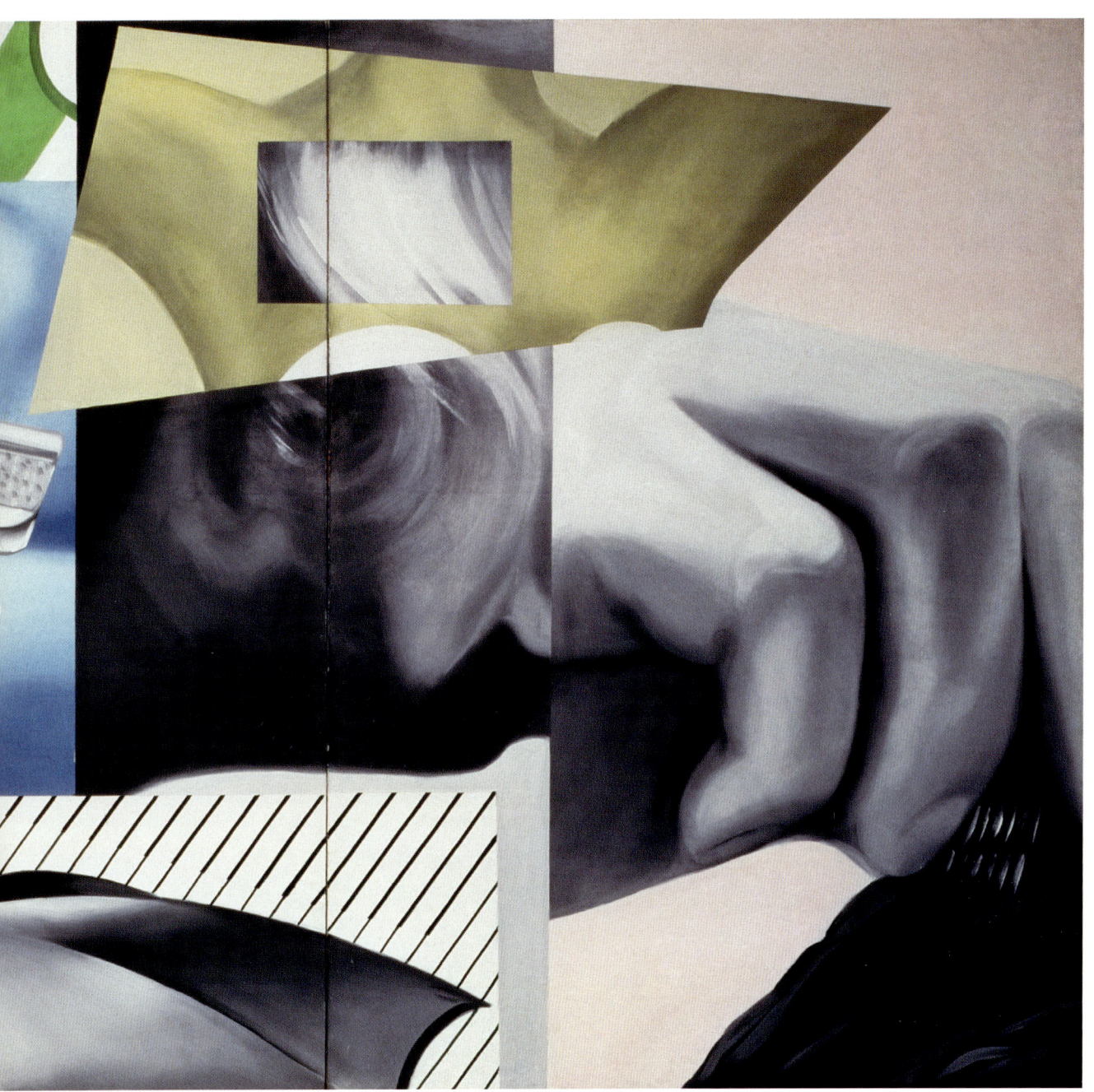

Portrait of the Scull Family

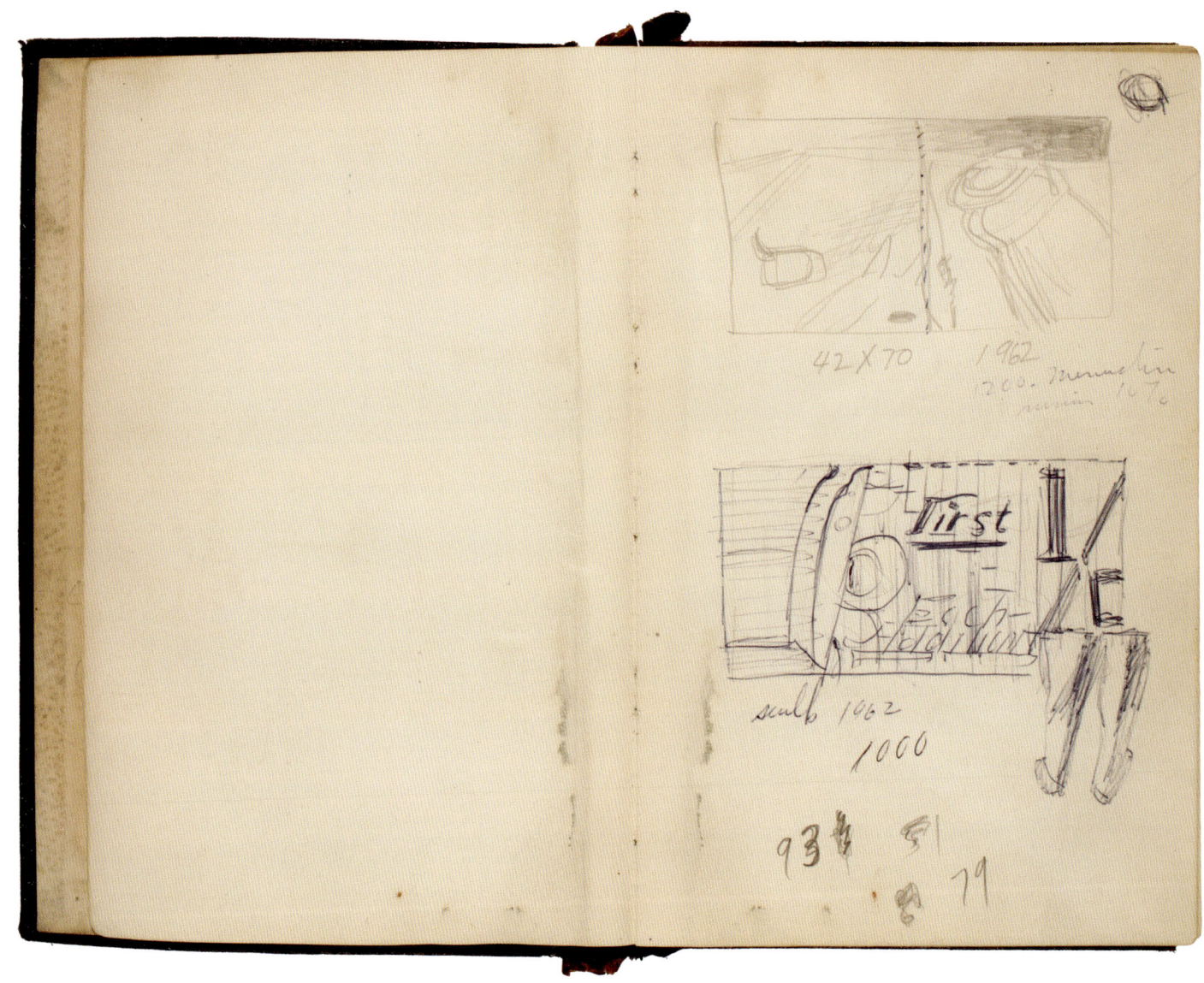

Ink sketch for *Portrait of the Scull Family* [lower image on recto]
From "Coenties Slip Sketchbook," ca. 1960–63
Graphite, ink, crayon, and colored pencil on paper (hardcover sketchbook)
8 1/2" x 5 1/2" (21.6 x 14.0 cm) [closed]; 8 1/2" x 11 1/2" (21.6 x 29.2 cm) [opened overall]
Collection of the Estate of James Rosenquist

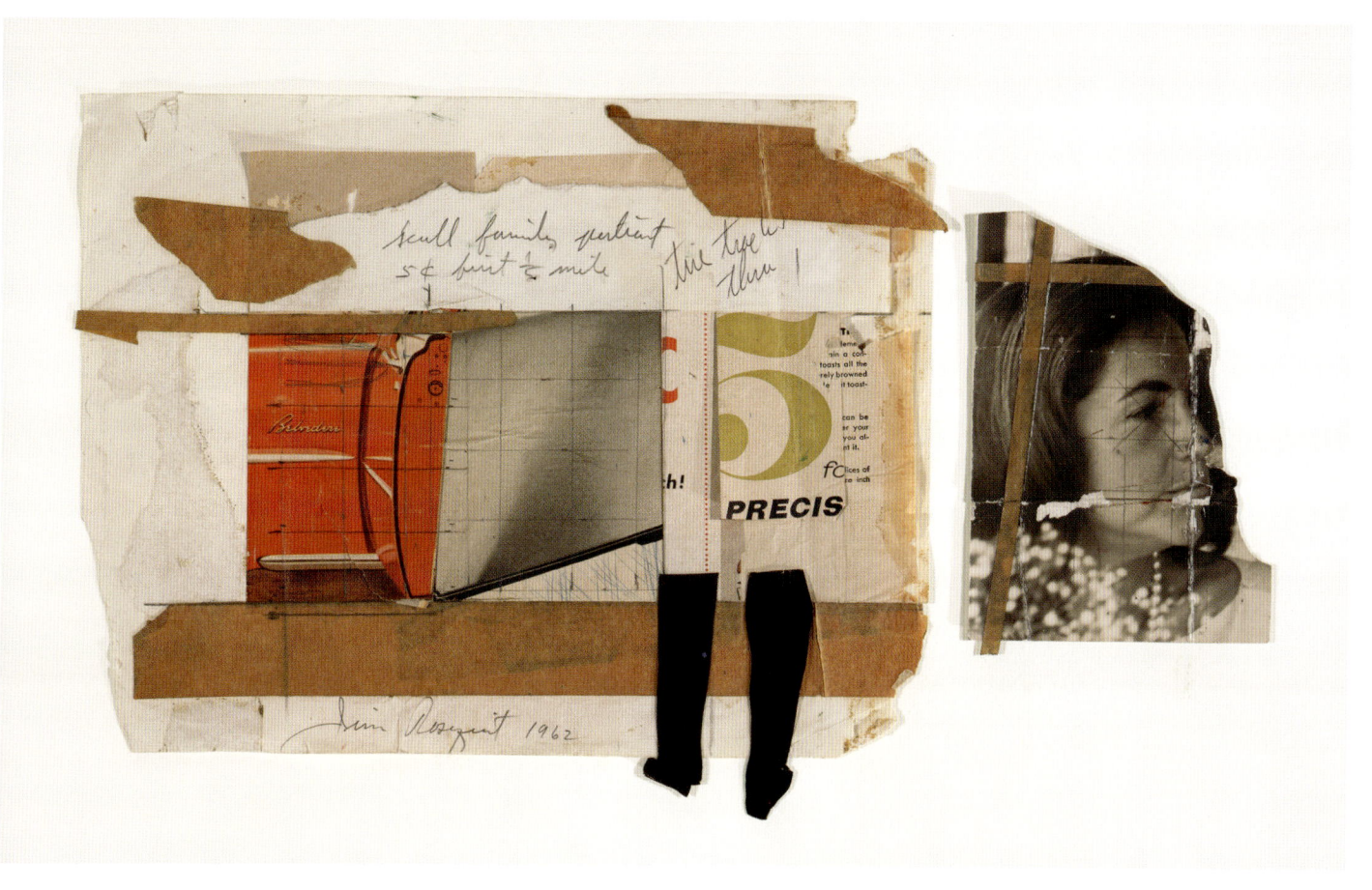

Source for *Portrait of the Scull Family,* 1962
Collage (magazine advertisement cutouts) and mixed media (paper, masking tape, colored pencil, graphite),
with adventitious marks, on paper; photograph with mixed media (masking tape, graphite)
9⁷/₈" x 12⁵/₁₆" (25.1 x 31.3 cm); 6¹/₁₆" x 4⁵/₁₆" (15.4 x 11.0 cm)
Presumed destroyed in Aripeka, Florida studio fire (April 25, 2009)

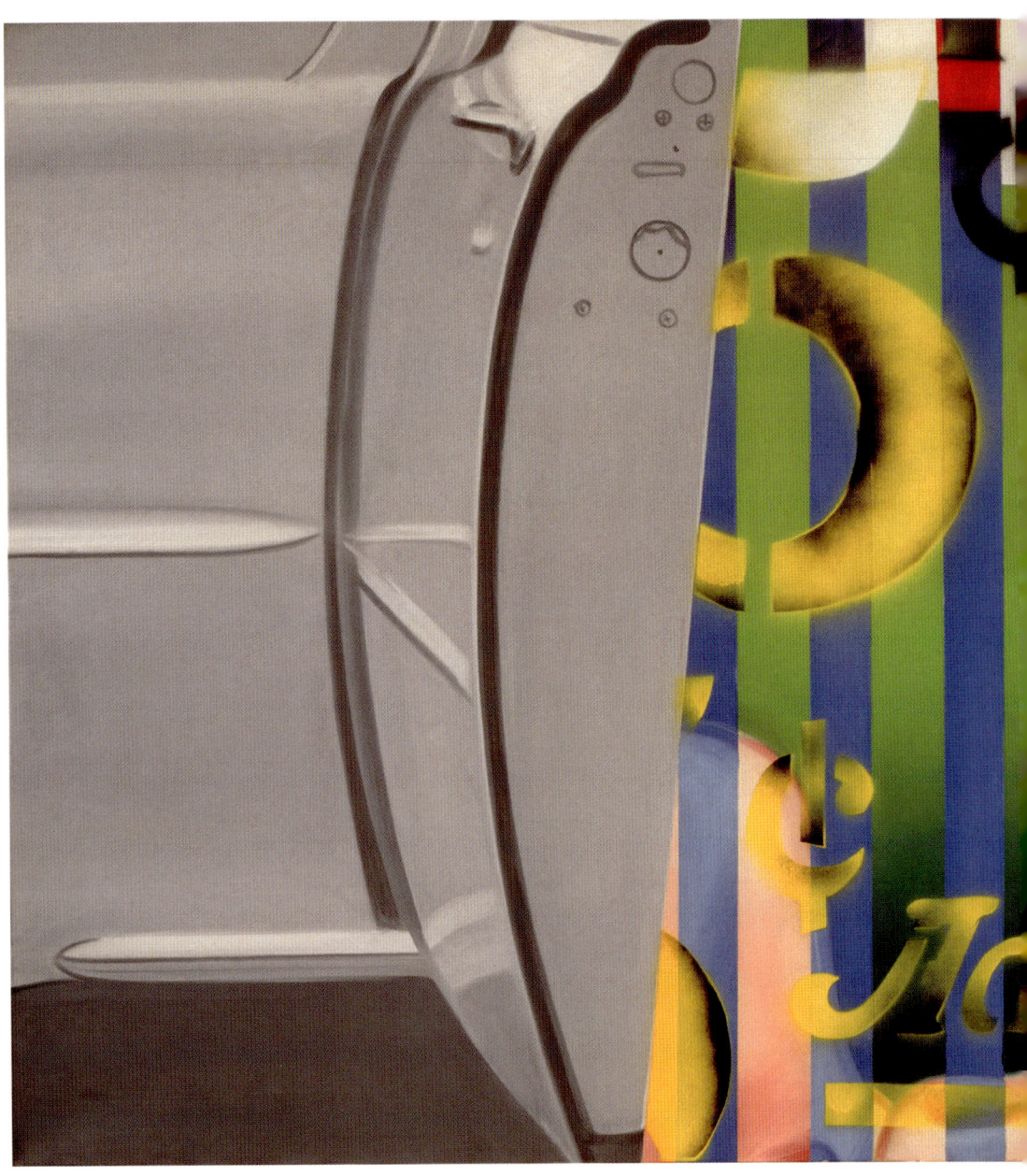

Portrait of the Scull Family, 1962
Oil on canvas and attached shaped panels
76³/₄" x 96" (194.9 x 243.8 cm)
Collection of Jane and Marc Nathanson

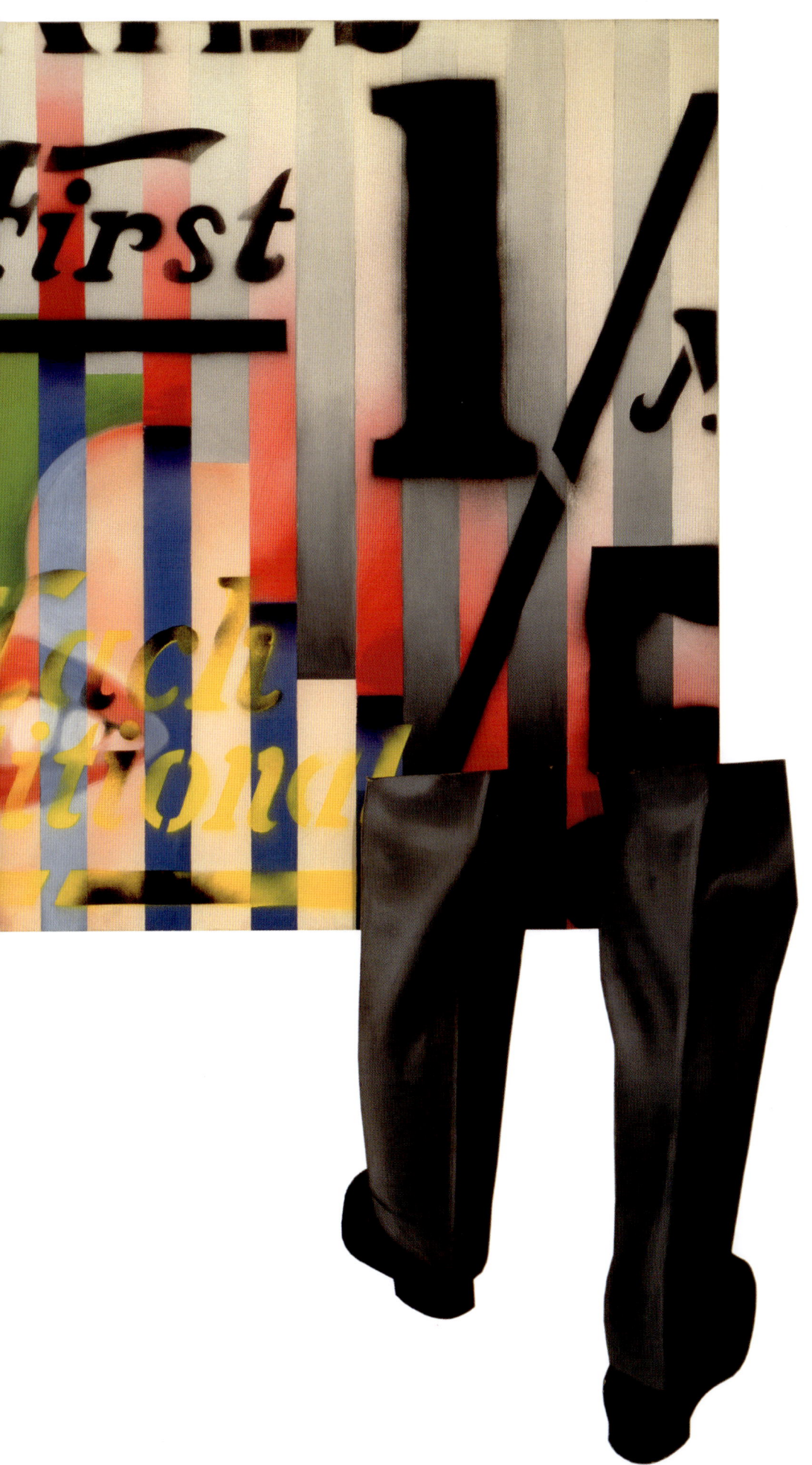

The Promenade of Merce Cunningham

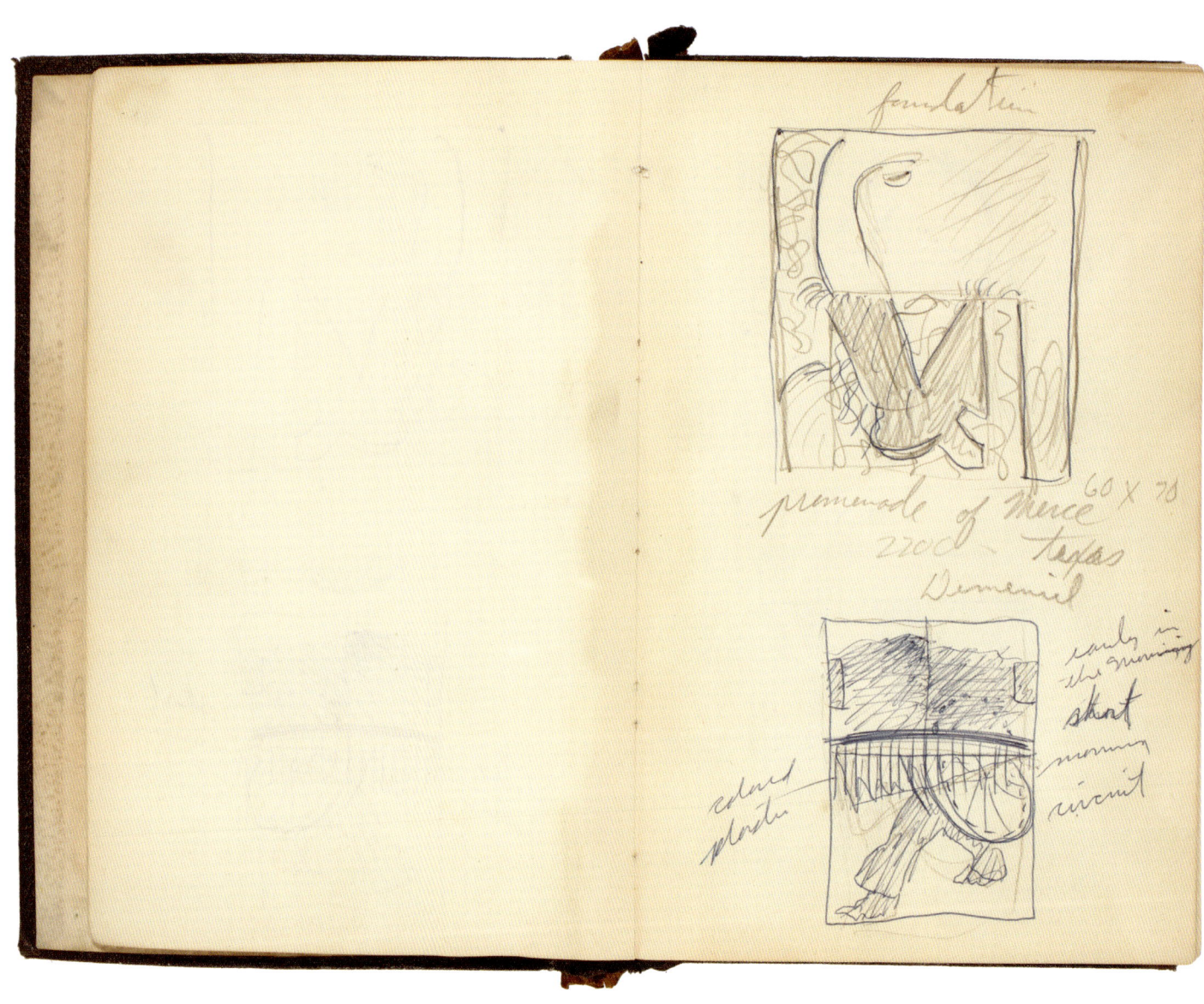

Pencil and ink sketch for *The Promenade of Merce Cunningham* [upper image on recto]
From "Coenties Slip Sketchbook," ca. 1960–63
Graphite, ink, crayon, and colored pencil on paper (hardcover sketchbook)
8 1/2" x 5 1/2" (21.6 x 14.0 cm) [closed]; 8 1/2" x 11 1/2" (21.6 x 29.2 cm) [opened overall]
Collection of the Estate of James Rosenquist

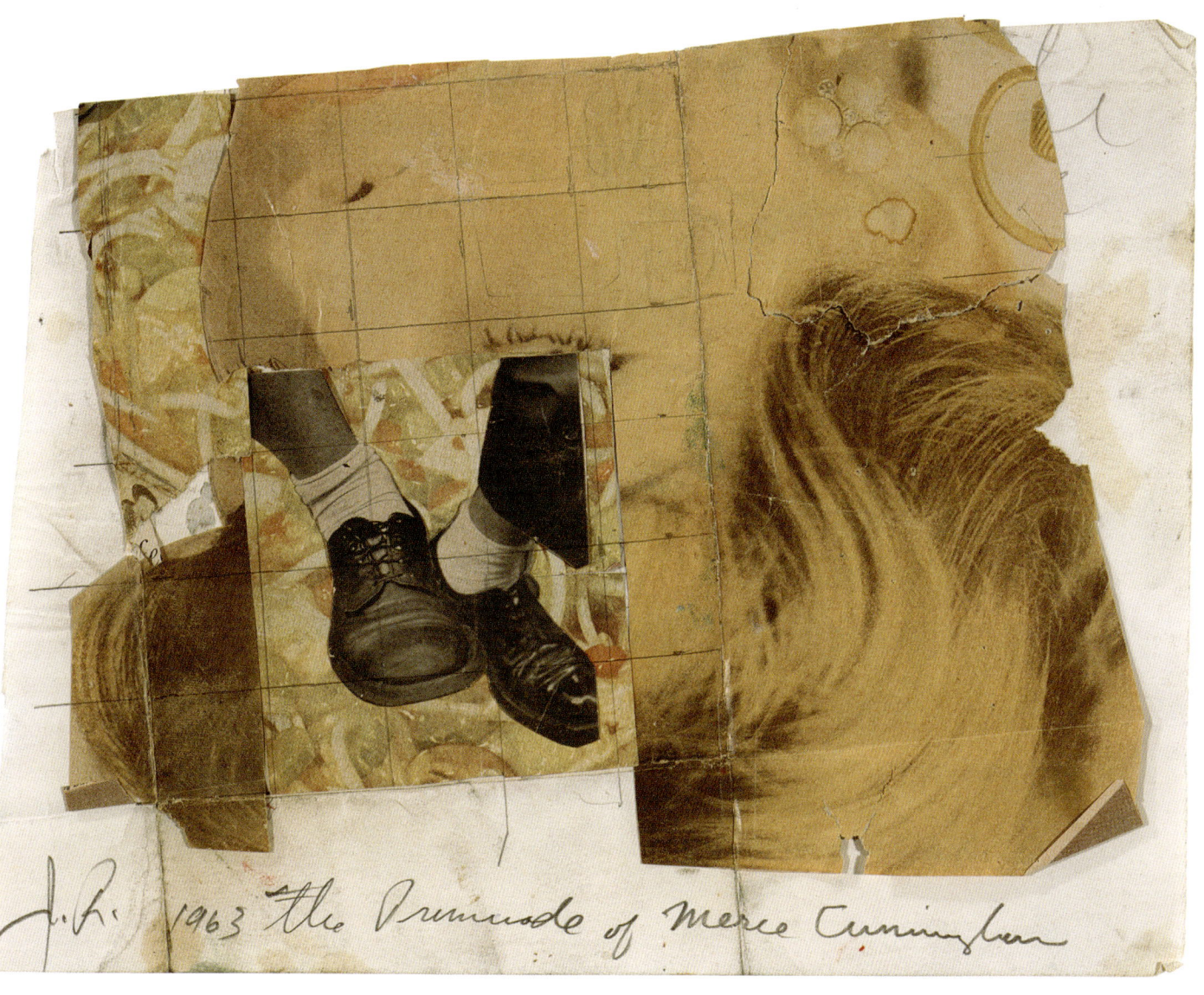

Source for *The Promenade of Merce Cunningham*, 1963
Collage (magazine advertisement cutouts) and graphite, with adventitious marks, on paper
7 1/2" x 9 3/4" (19.1 x 24.8 cm)
Collection of the Estate of James Rosenquist

The Promenade of Merce Cunningham, 1963
Oil on canvas
70" x 60" (177.8 x 152.4 cm)
The Menil Collection, Houston, Formerly in the collection of Christophe de Menil [Z 601]

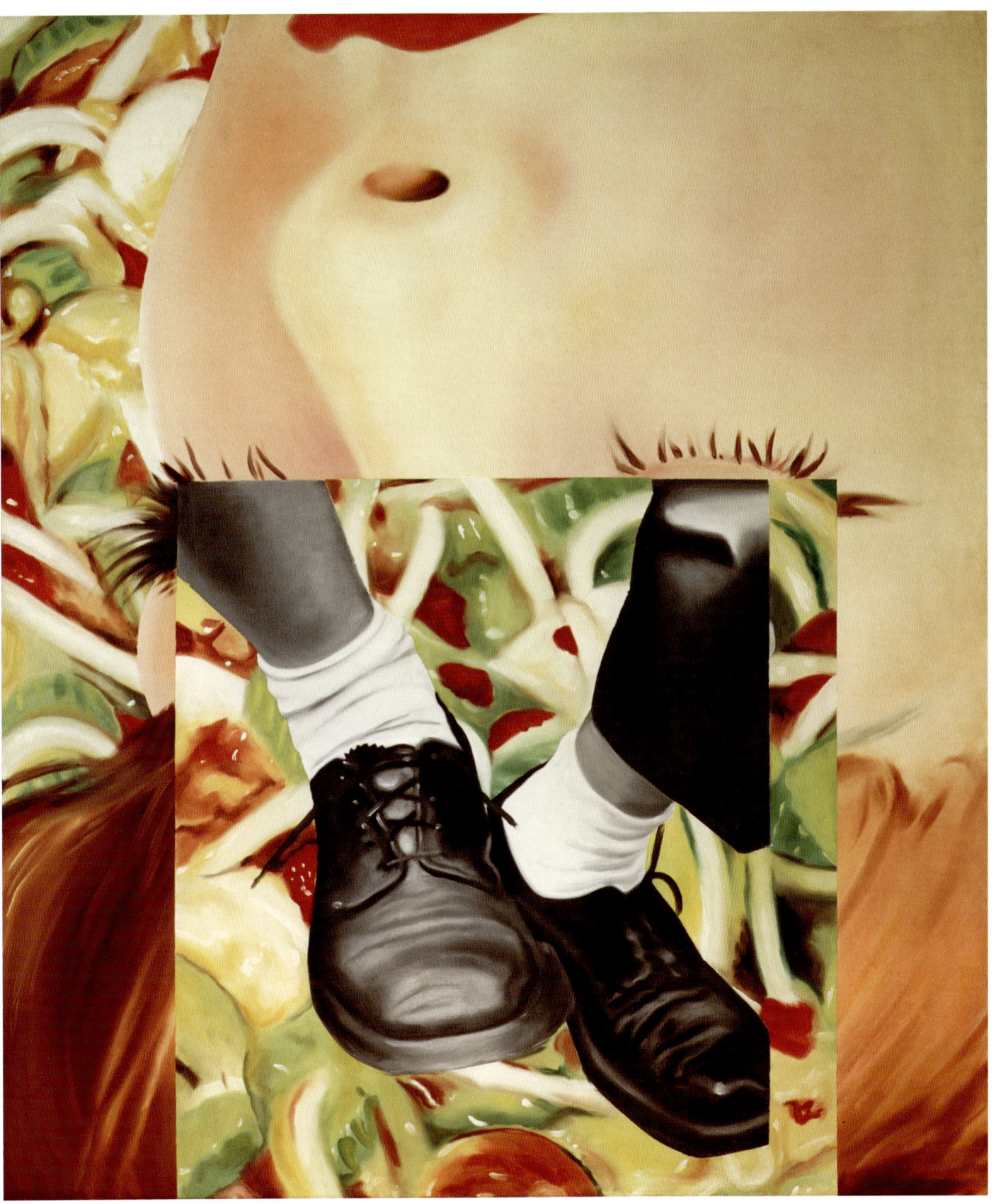

Horse Blinders

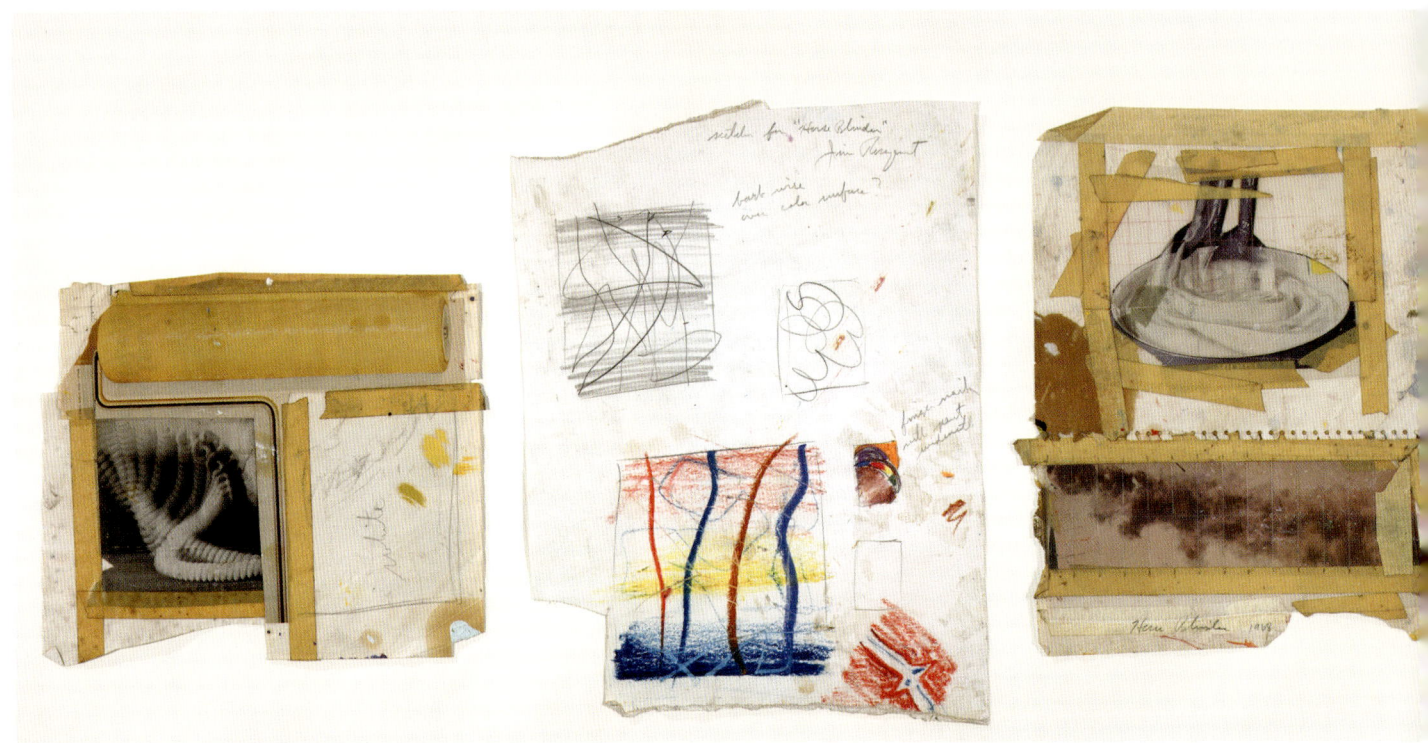

Sources and Preparatory Studies for *Horse Blinders*, 1967–68
Collage (magazine advertisement cutouts, advertising reproduction) and mixed media
(masking tape, incised plastic film with rubbed-in paint, incised plastic film, paint, graphite, crayon), with adventitious marks, on paper
Overall dimensions: 19" x 83" (48.3 x 210.8 cm) [approx.]
Collection of the Estate of James Rosenquist

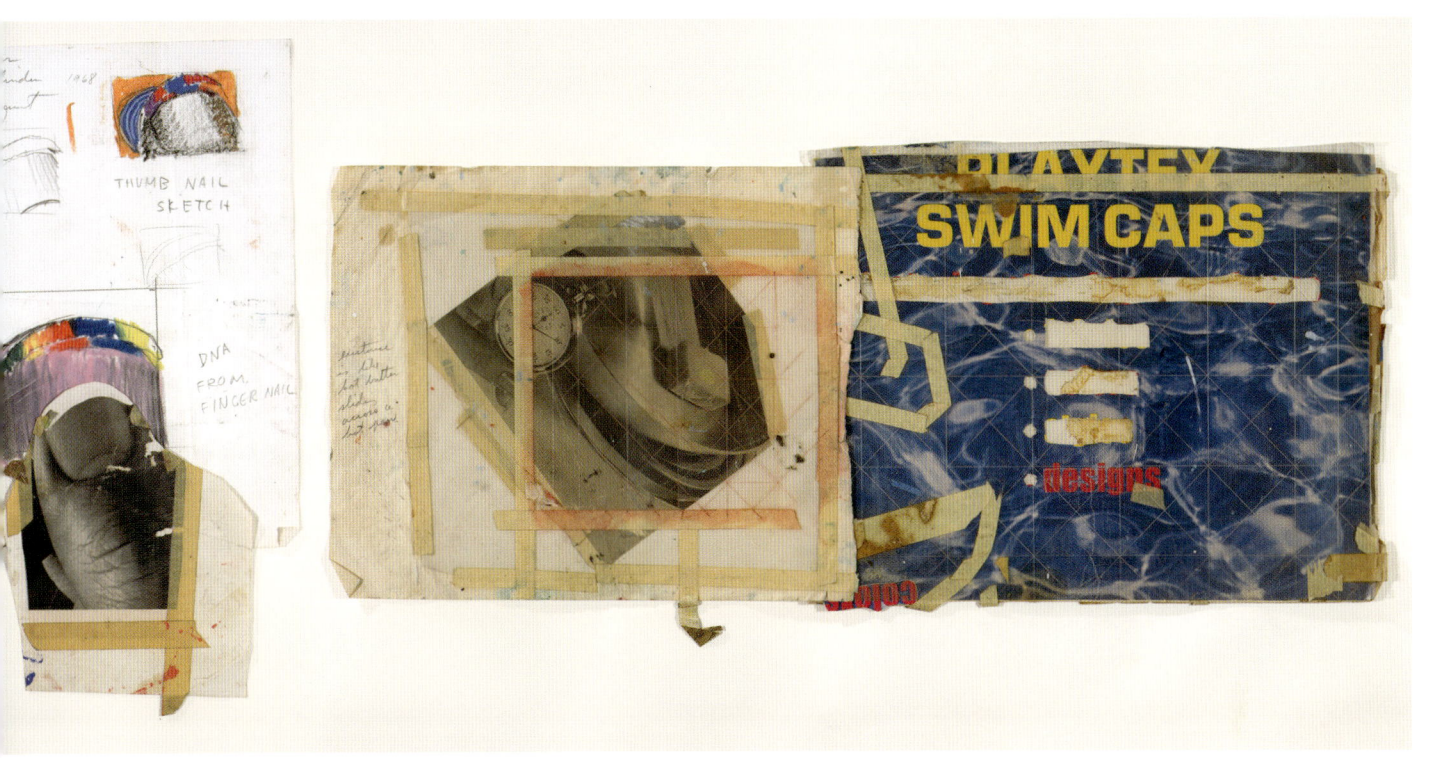

76

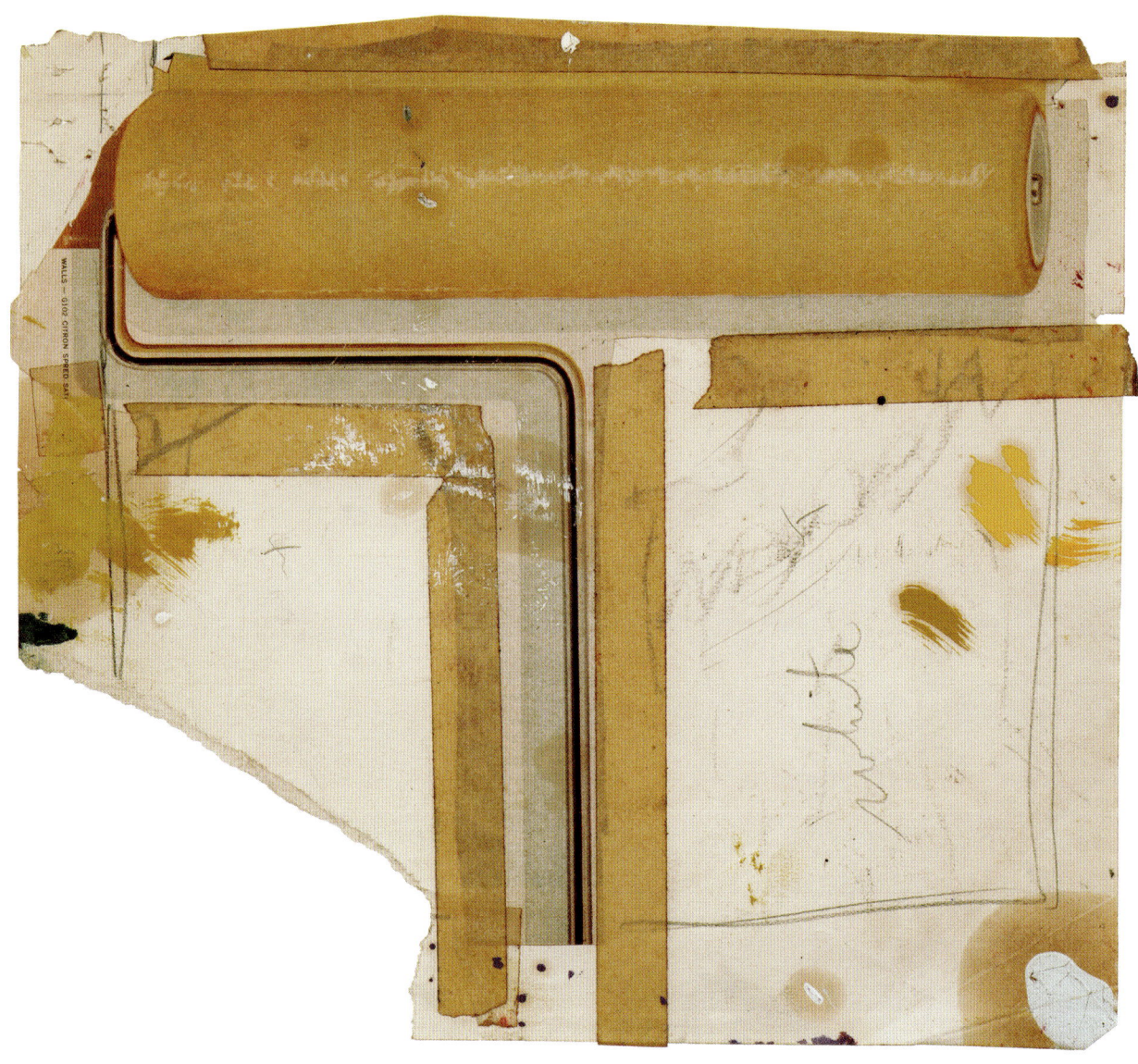

Original *Horse Blinders* source element, 1968
(subsequently combined by the artist with other *Horse Blinders* elements and studies; illus. pp. 74–75)
Magazine advertisement cutout, masking tape, graphite, and paint, with adventitious marks, on paper
10 3/4" x 12 3/16" (27.3 x 31.0 cm) [approx.]

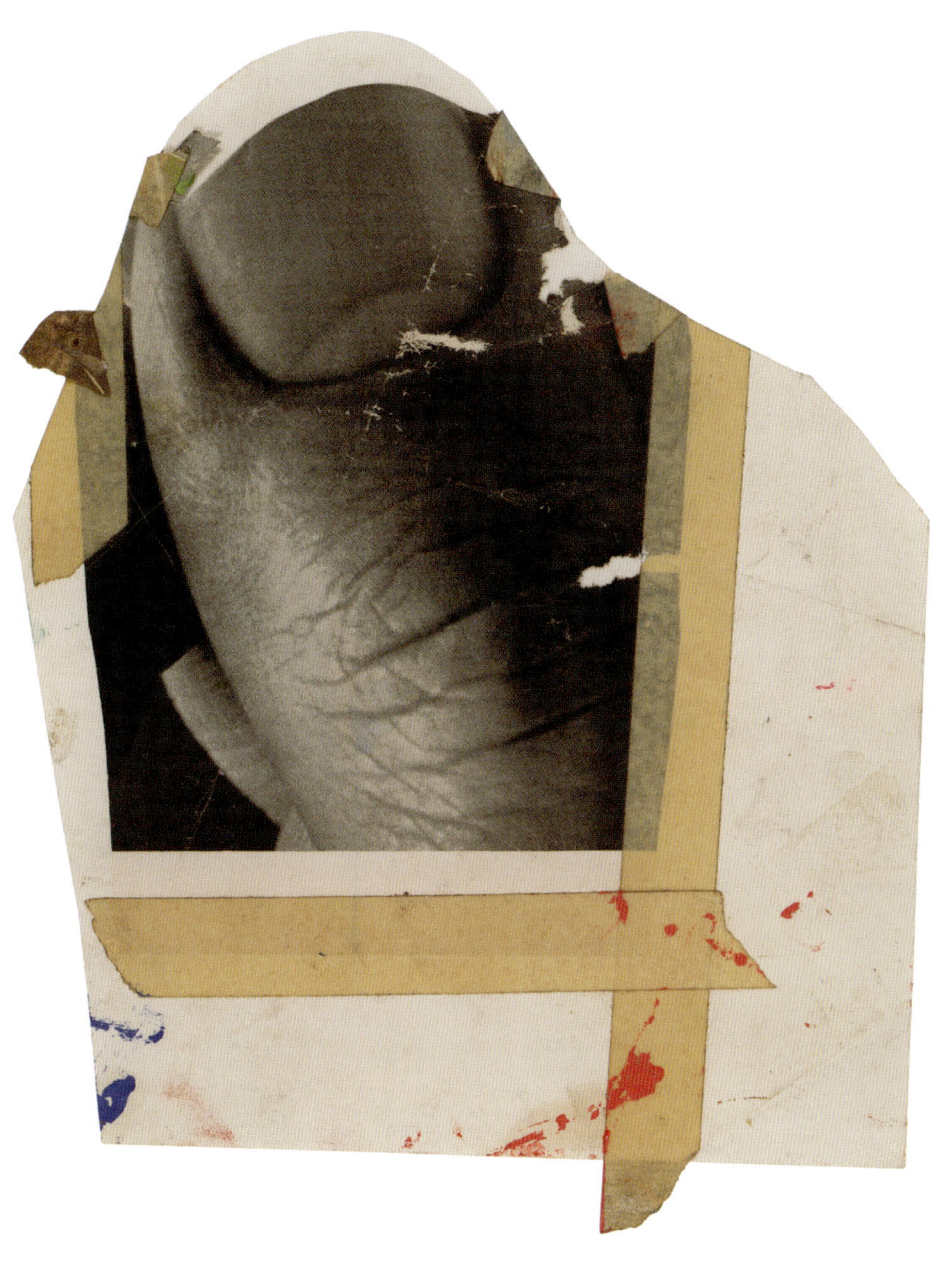

Original *Horse Blinders* source element, 1968
(subsequently combined by the artist with other *Horse Blinders* elements and studies; illus. pp. 74–75)
Magazine advertisement cutout and masking tape, with adventitious marks, on paper
9 3/16" x 7 3/16" (23.3 x 18.3 cm) [approx.]

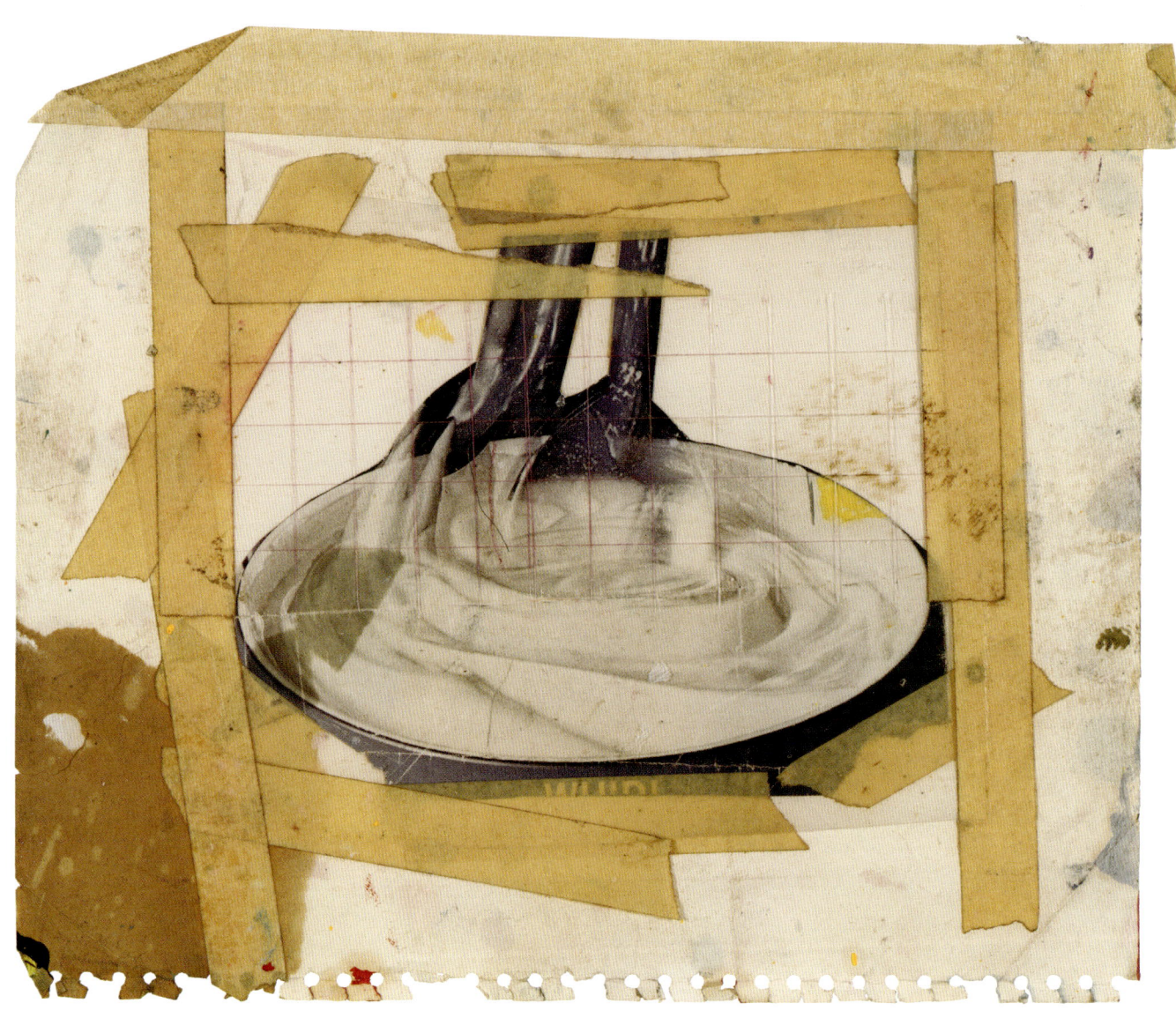

Original *Horse Blinders* source element, 1968
(subsequently combined by the artist with other *Horse Blinders* elements and studies; illus. pp. 74–75)
Magazine advertisement cutout, incised plastic film with rubbed-in paint, and masking tape, with adventitious marks, on paper
9 1/4" x 11 5/16" (23.5 x 28.7 cm) [approx.]

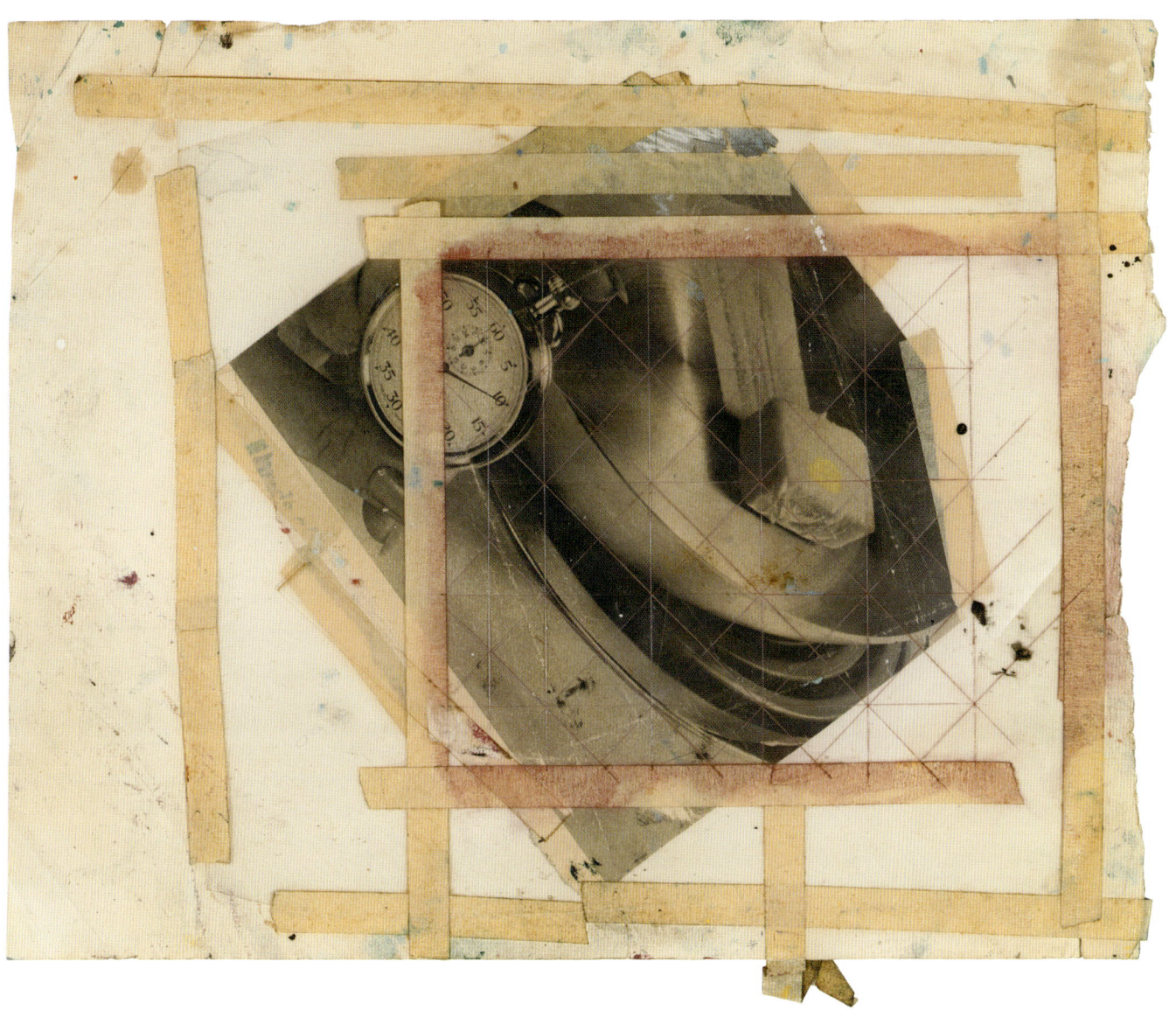

Original *U-Haul-It* and *Horse Blinders* source element, 1967
(subsequently combined by the artist with other *Horse Blinders* elements and studies; illus. pp. 74–75)
Magazine advertisement cutout, incised plastic film with rubbed-in paint, and masking tape, with adventitious marks, on paper
12$^7/_{16}$" x 15$^3/_{16}$" (31.6 x 38.6 cm) [approx.]

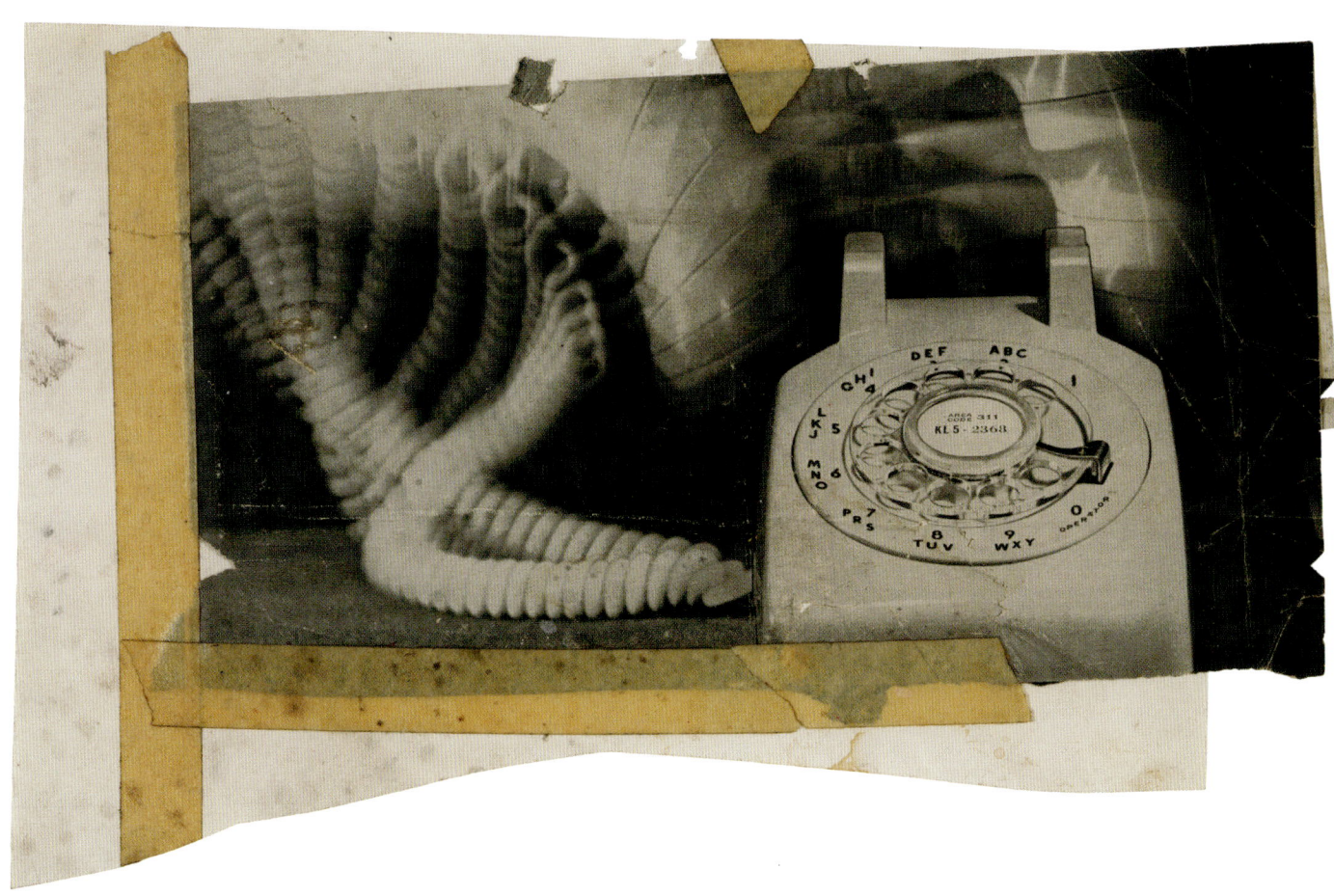

Original *Horse Blinders* source element, 1968
(subsequently combined by the artist with other *Horse Blinders* elements and studies; illus. pp. 74–75)
Magazine advertisement cutout and masking tape, with adventitious marks, on paper
7 11/16" x 12 1/8" (19.5 x 30.8 cm) [approx.]

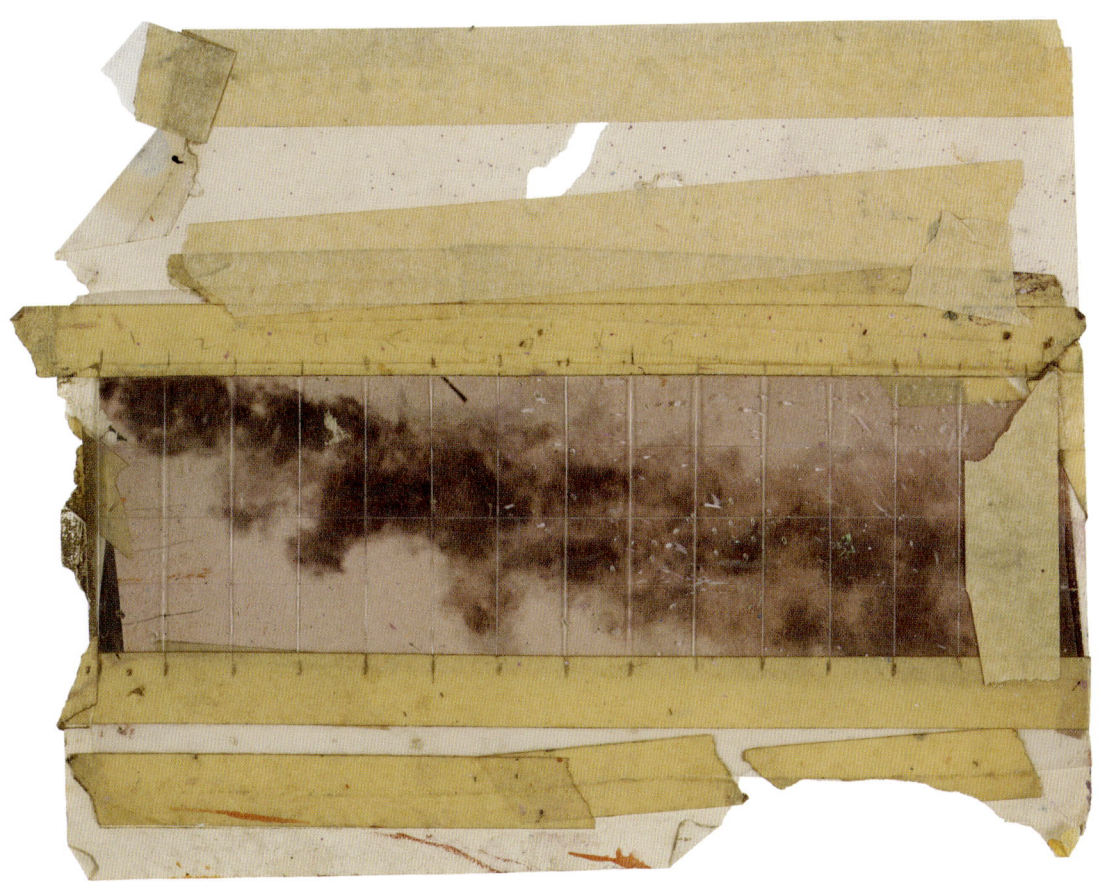

Original *Horse Blinders* source element, 1968
(subsequently combined by the artist with other *Horse Blinders* elements and studies; illus. pp. 74–75)
Magazine illustration cutout, incised plastic film, and masking tape, with adventitious marks, on paper
9" x 11^{11}/$_{16}$" (22.9 x 29.7 cm) [approx.]

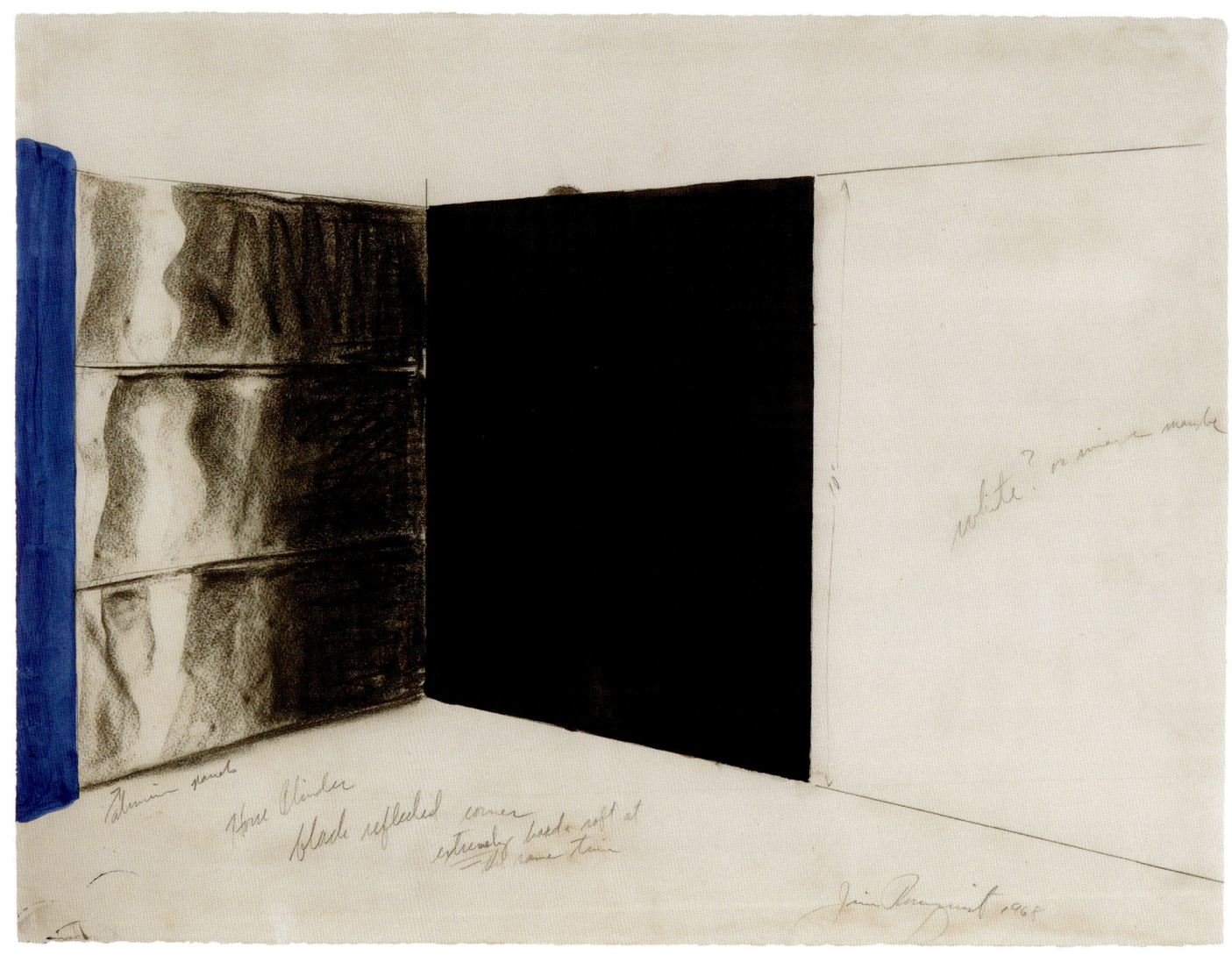

Sketch for Horse Blinders (Black Reflected Corner), 1968
Watercolor, charcoal, and graphite on paper
22 ¹⁄₂" x 29 ¹⁄₂" (57.2 x 74.9 cm)
Private Collection

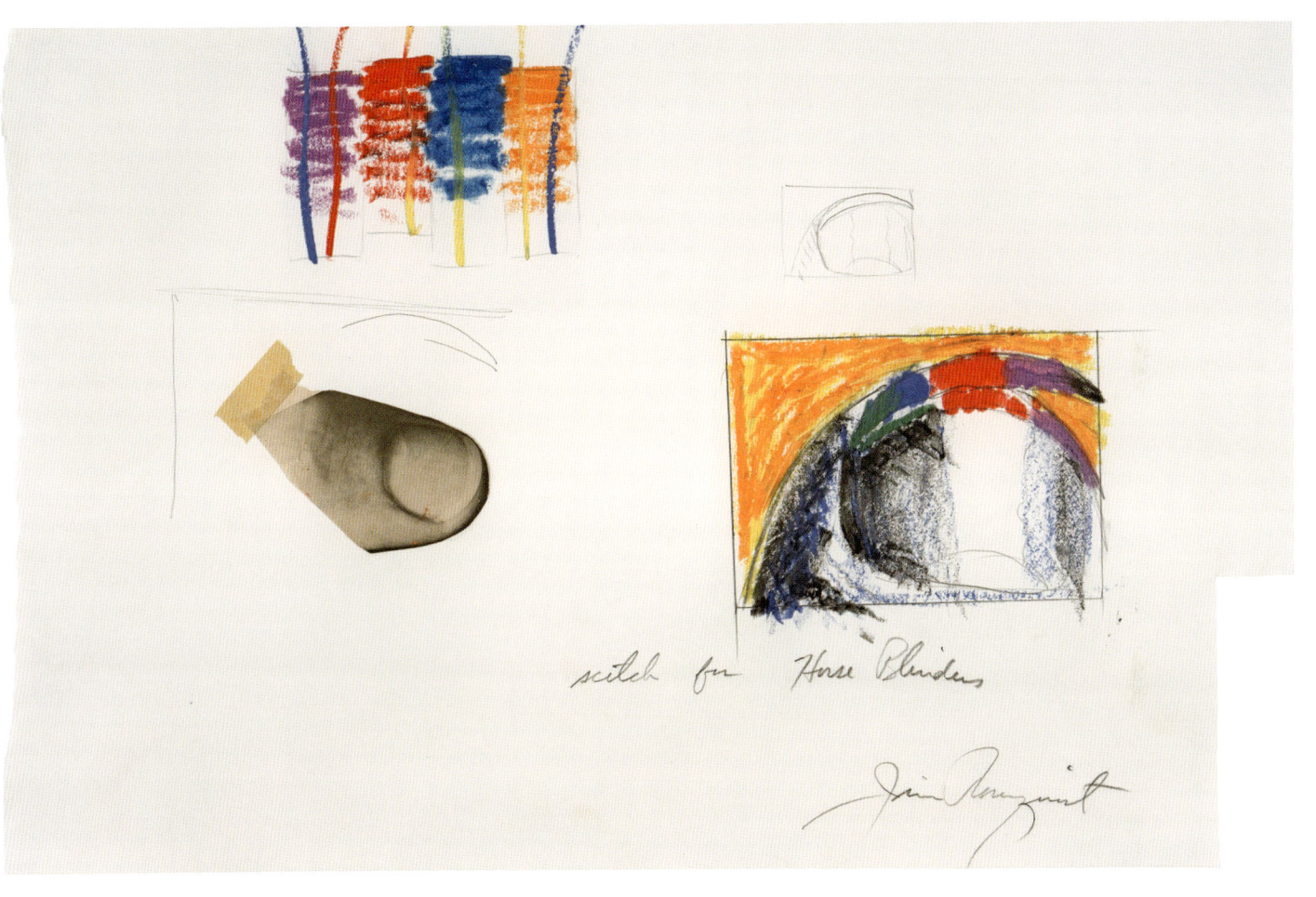

scitch for Horse Blinders

Sketch for Horse Blinders, circa 1968
Crayon, graphite, masking tape, and collage (magazine advertisement cutout) on paper
14" x 22 $^1/_{16}$" (35.6 x 56.0 cm)
Collection of the Estate of James Rosenquist

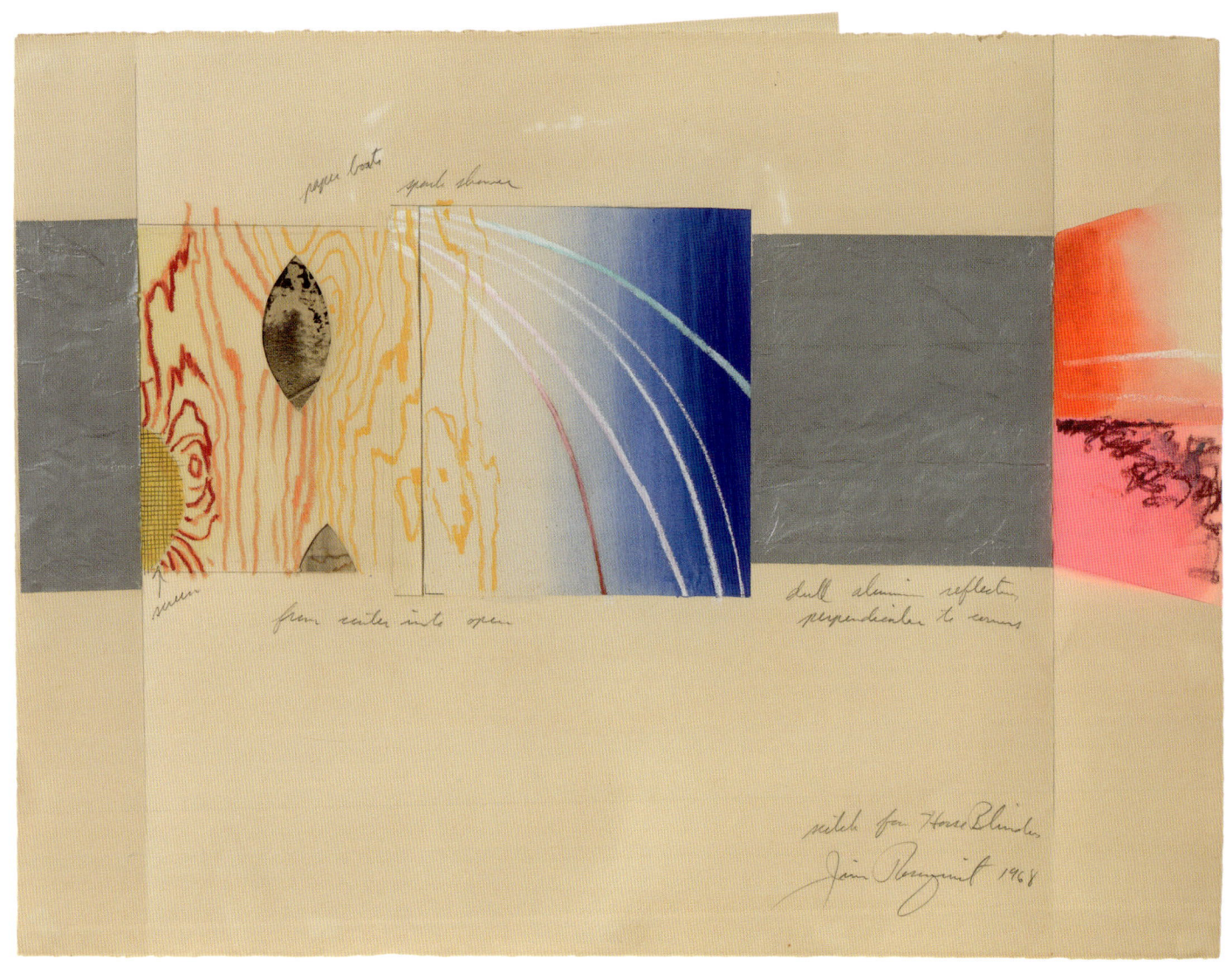

Sketch for Horse Blinders, 1968
Watercolor, pastel, graphite, aluminum foil, and paper collage on paper
22¼" x 30" (56.5 x 76.2 cm)
Private Collection

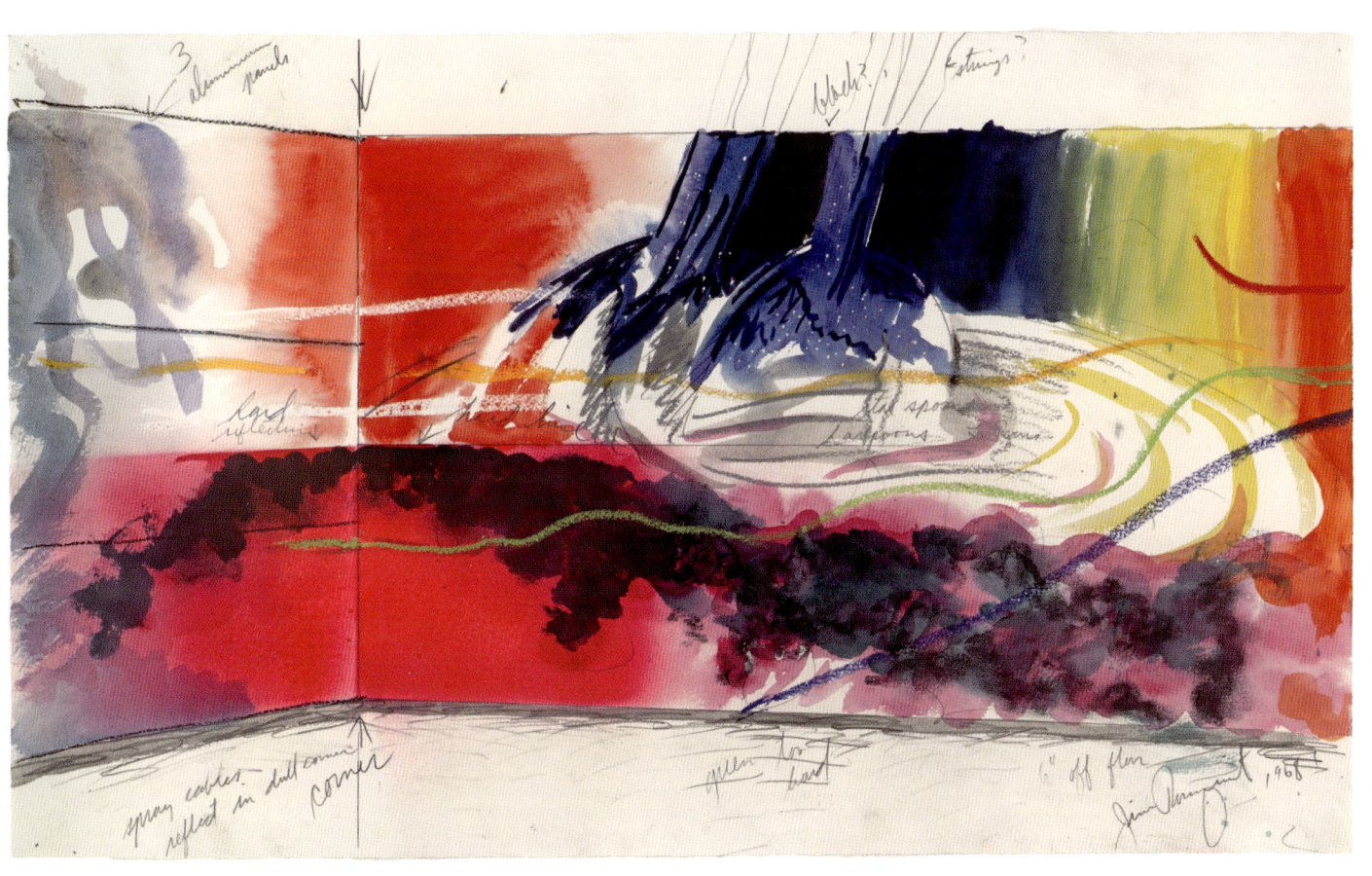

Sketch for Horse Blinders (Star Spoons), 1968
Watercolor, graphite, and crayon on paper
17 ½" x 29 ¾" (44.5 x 75.6 cm)
Private Collection

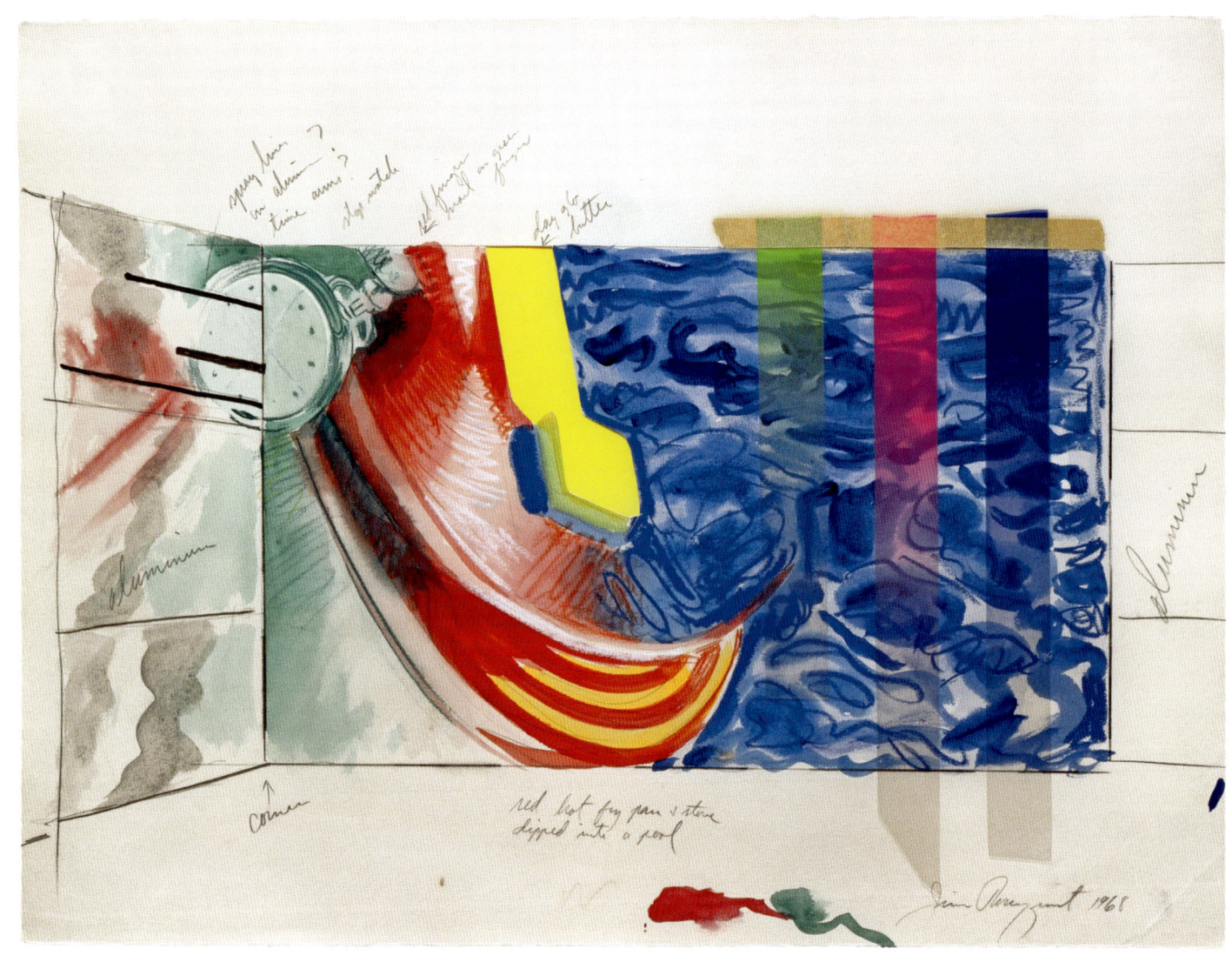

Sketch for Horse Blinders (Butter as Existence, Melting across a Hot Pan), 1968
Collage, watercolor, painted plastic, and masking tape on paper
22 ¼" x 30" (56.5 x 76.2 cm)
Private Collection

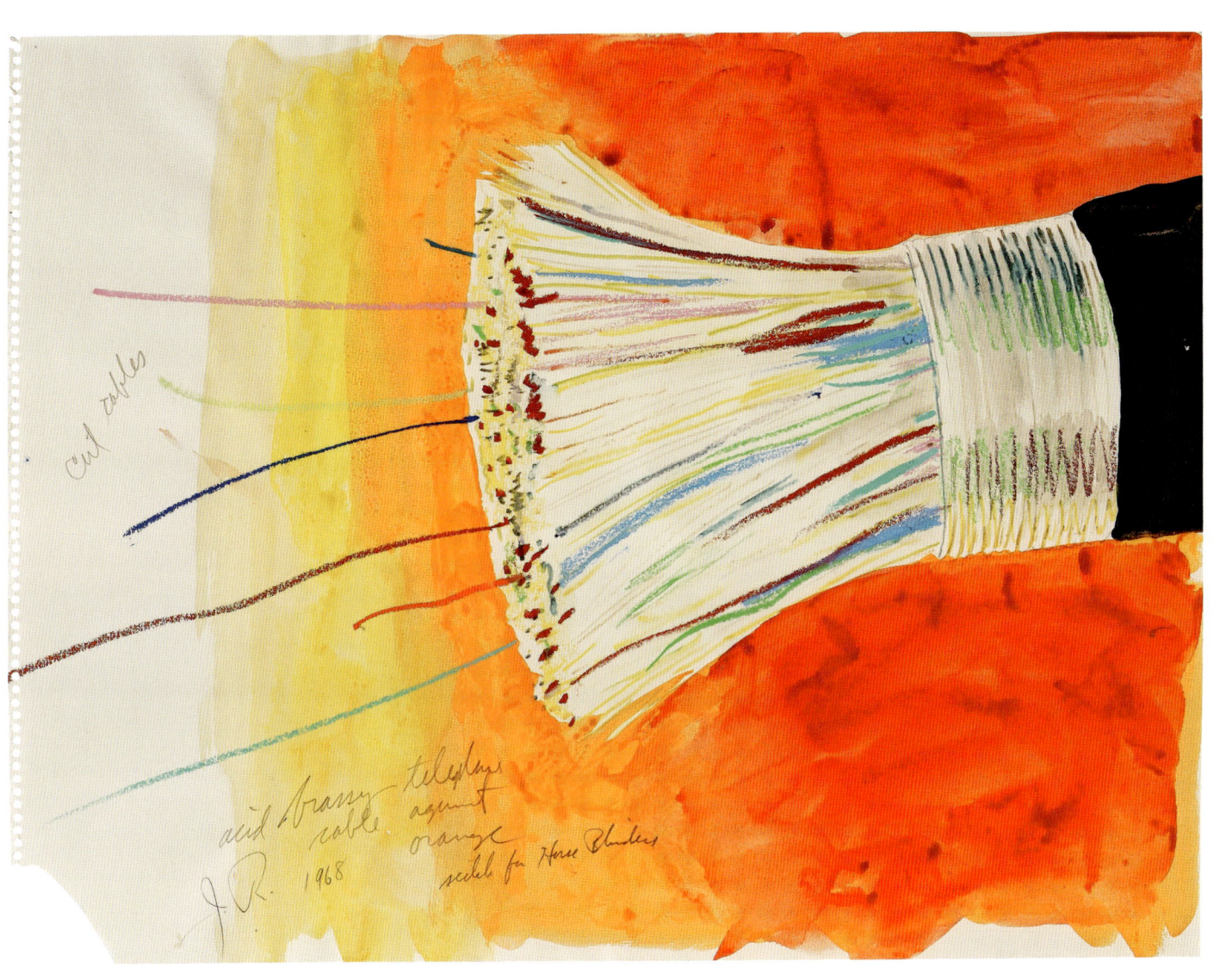

Sketch for Horse Blinders, 1968
Watercolor and crayon on paper
23" x 29" (58.4 x 73.7 cm)
Private Collection

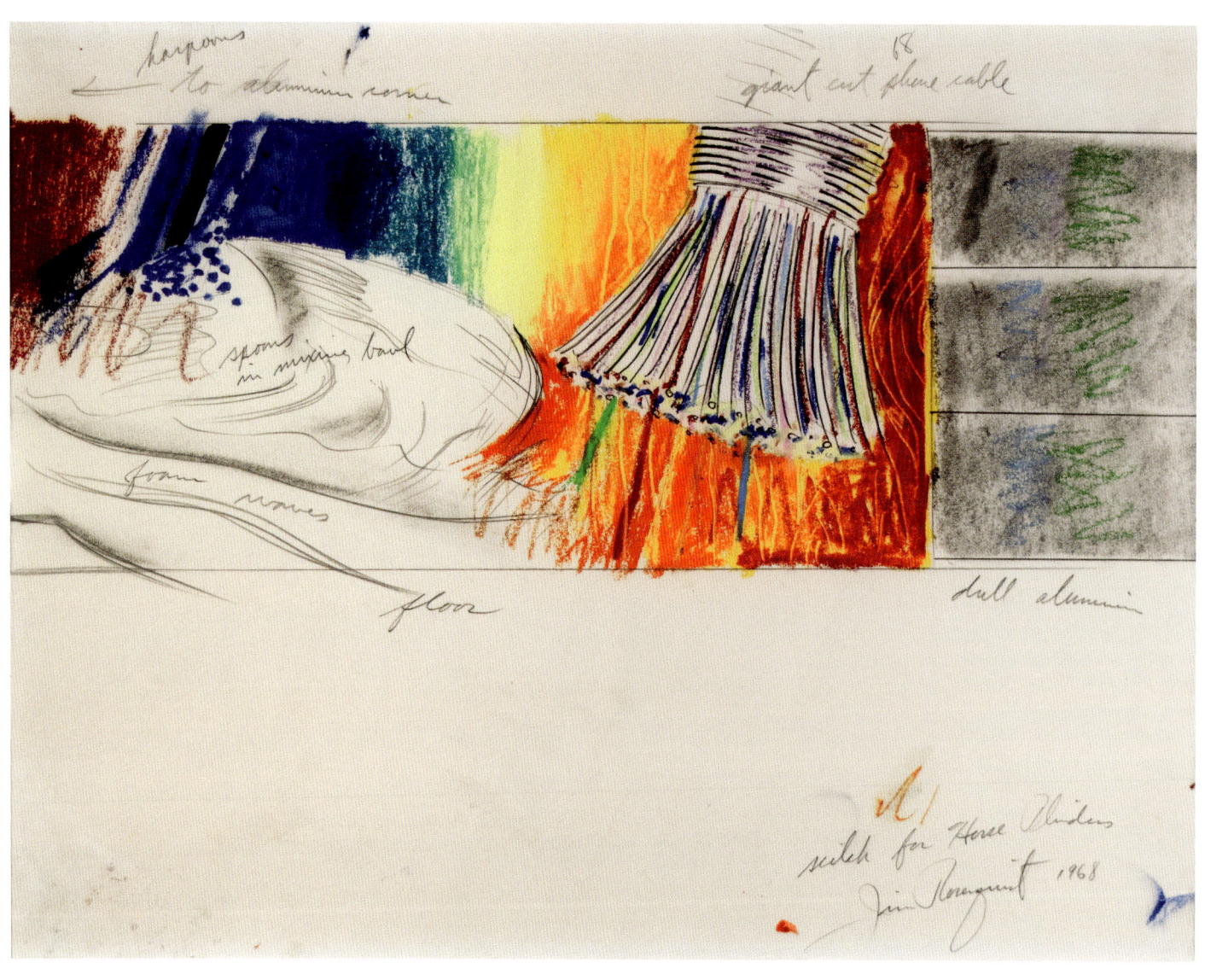

Sketch for Horse Blinders, 1968
Mixed media on paper
18" x 26" (45.7 x 66.0 cm)
Private Collection

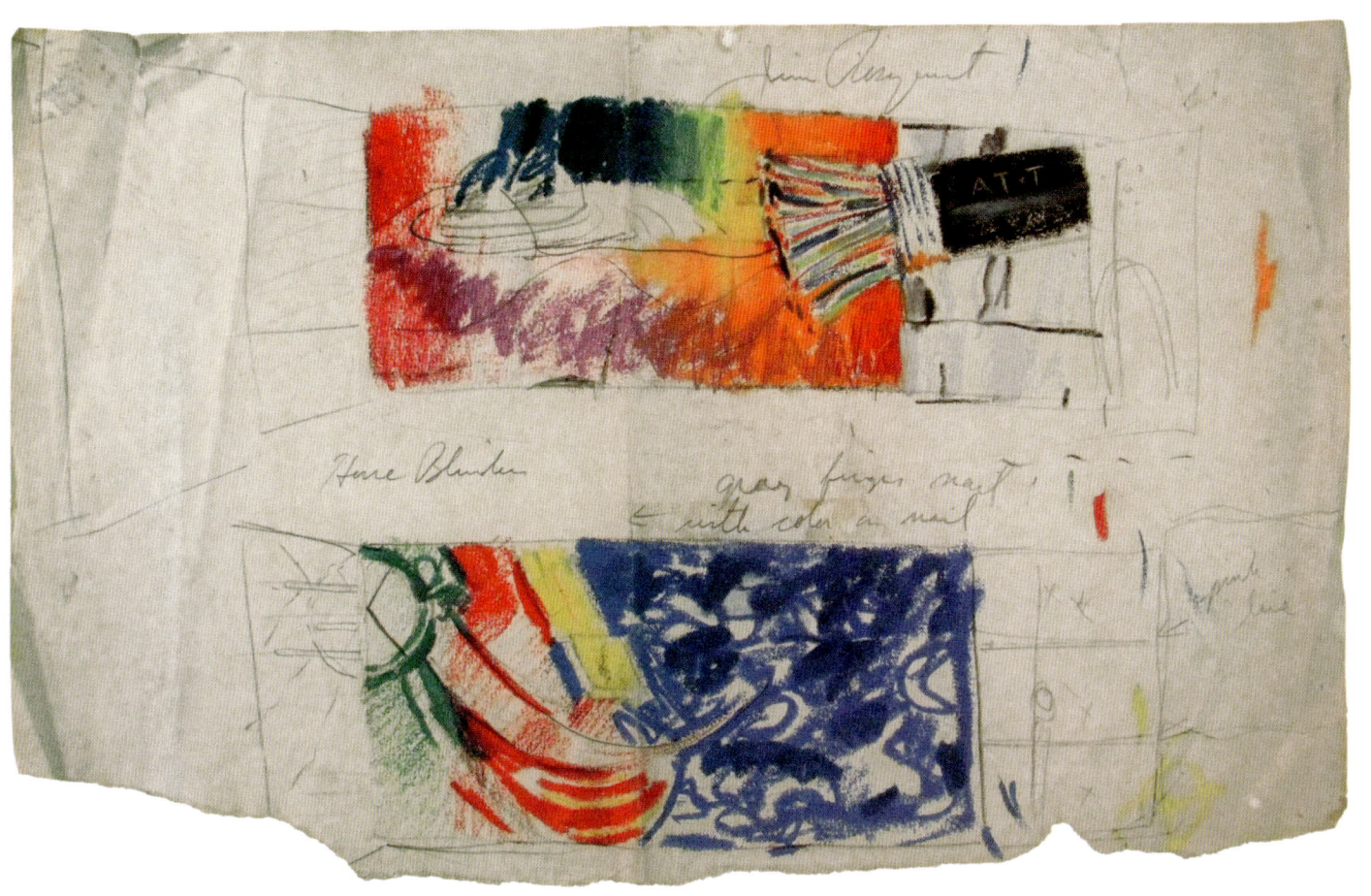

Horse Blinders, circa 1968
Crayon and graphite on paper
10 $^{15}/_{16}$" x 17 $^{15}/_{16}$" (27.8 x 45.6 cm)
Presumed destroyed in Aripeka, Florida studio fire (April 25, 2009)

90

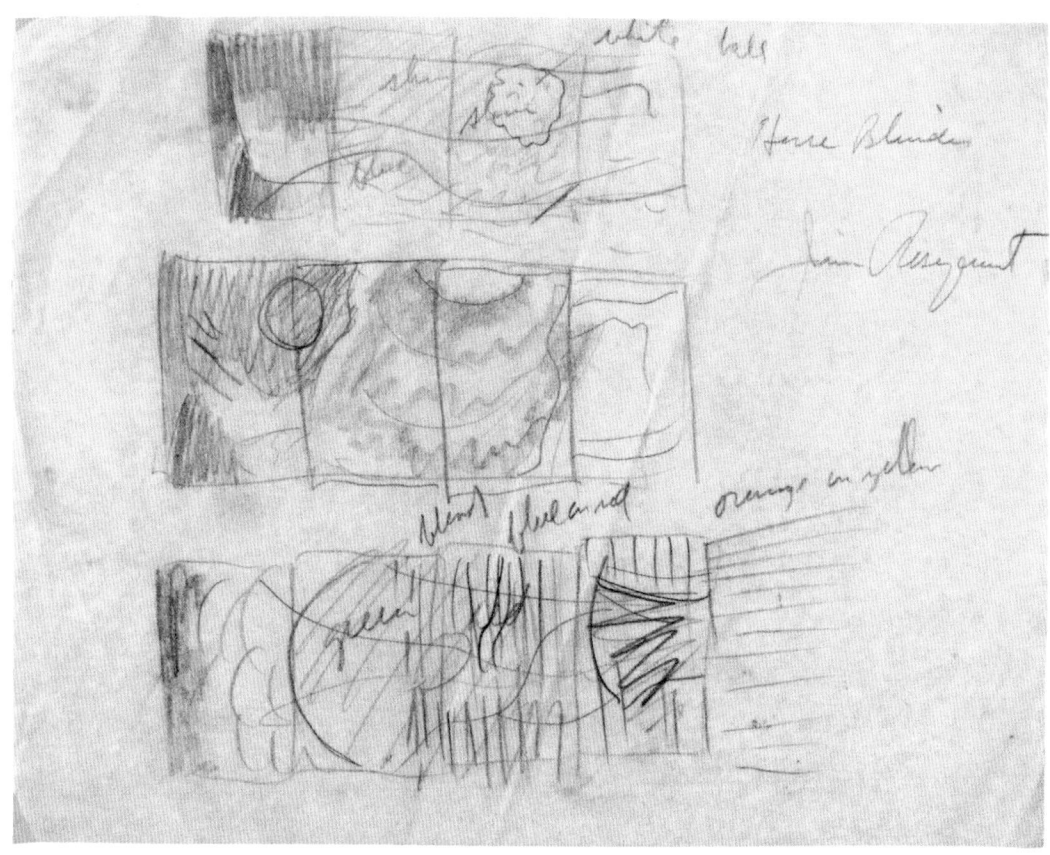

Horse Blinders, circa 1968
Graphite on paper
8 7/16" x 11" (21.4 x 27.9 cm)
Presumed destroyed in Aripeka, Florida studio fire (April 25, 2009)

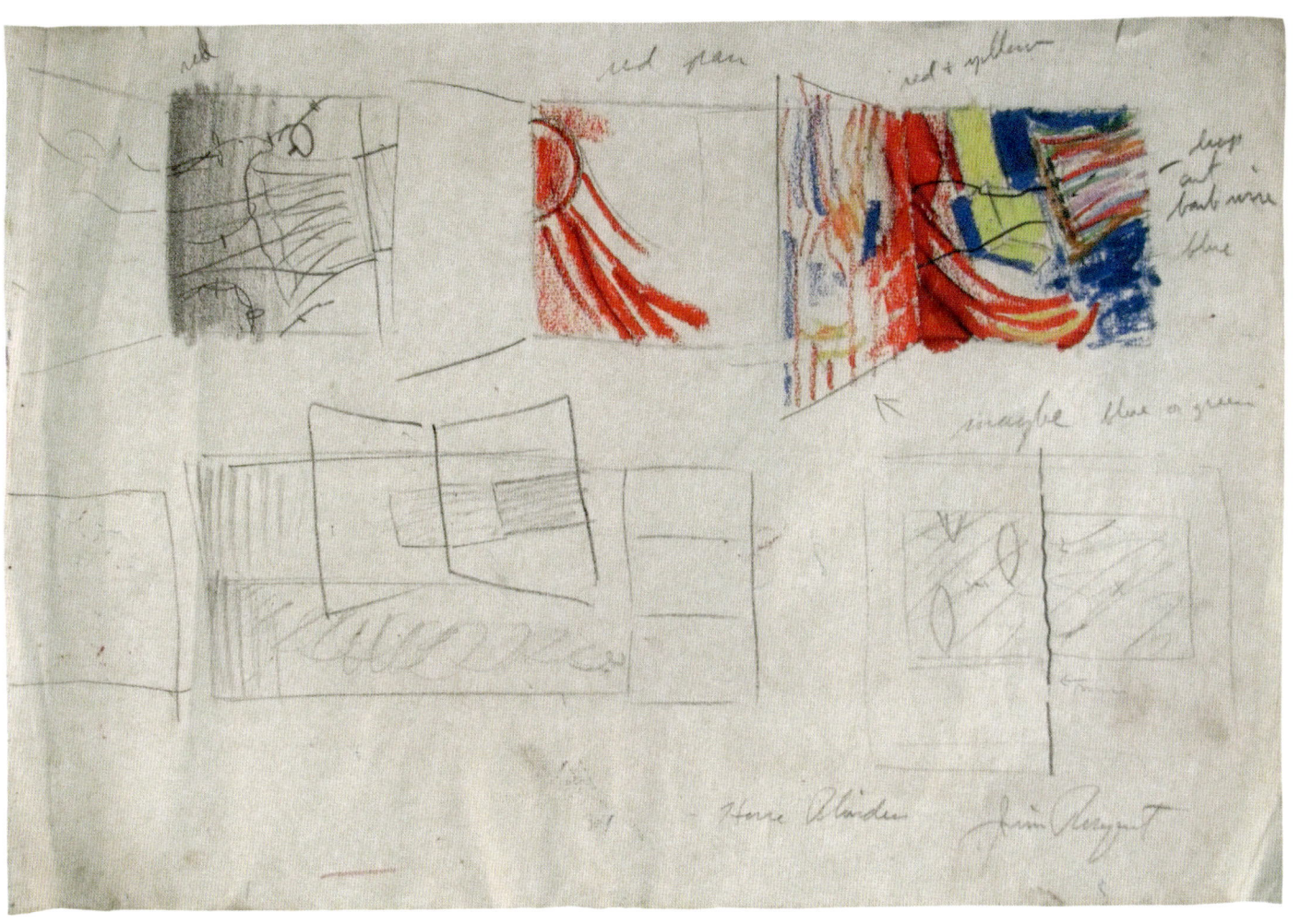

Horse Blinders, circa 1968
Crayon and graphite on paper
11 15/16" x 17 15/16" (30.3 x 45.6 cm)
Presumed destroyed in Aripeka, Florida studio fire (April 25, 2009)

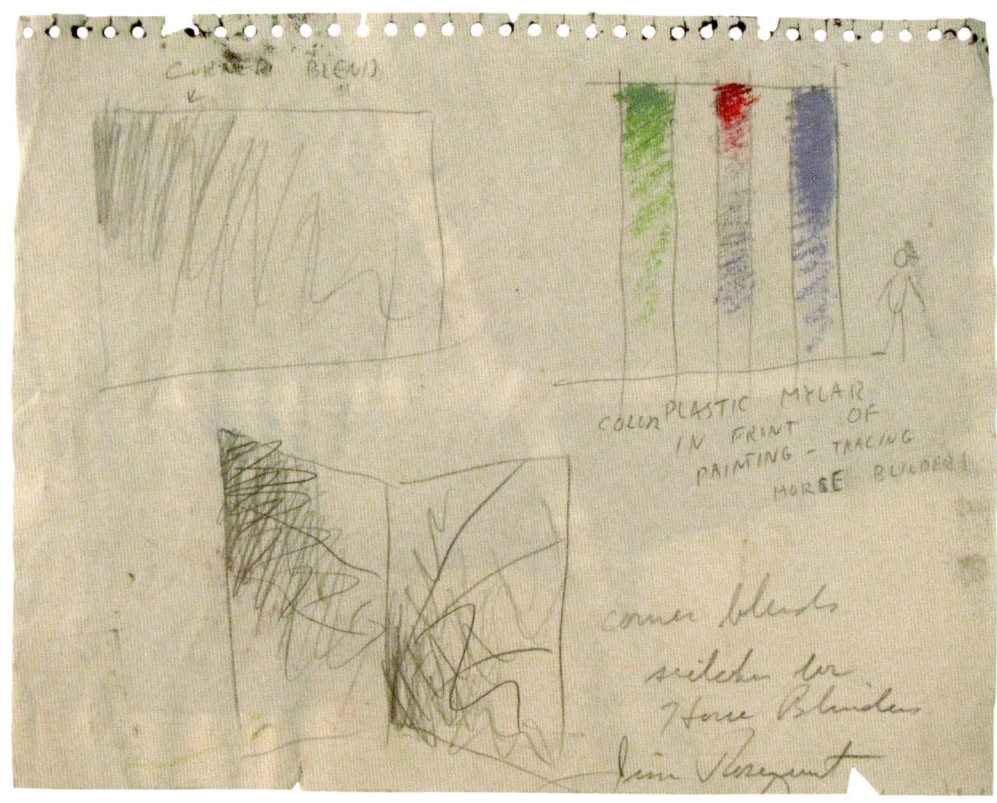

Sketches for Horse Blinders, circa 1968
Graphite and crayon on paper (with black ink on verso)
8 $^{7}/_{16}$" x 10 $^{11}/_{16}$" (21.4 x 27.2 cm)
Presumed destroyed in Aripeka, Florida studio fire (April 25, 2009)

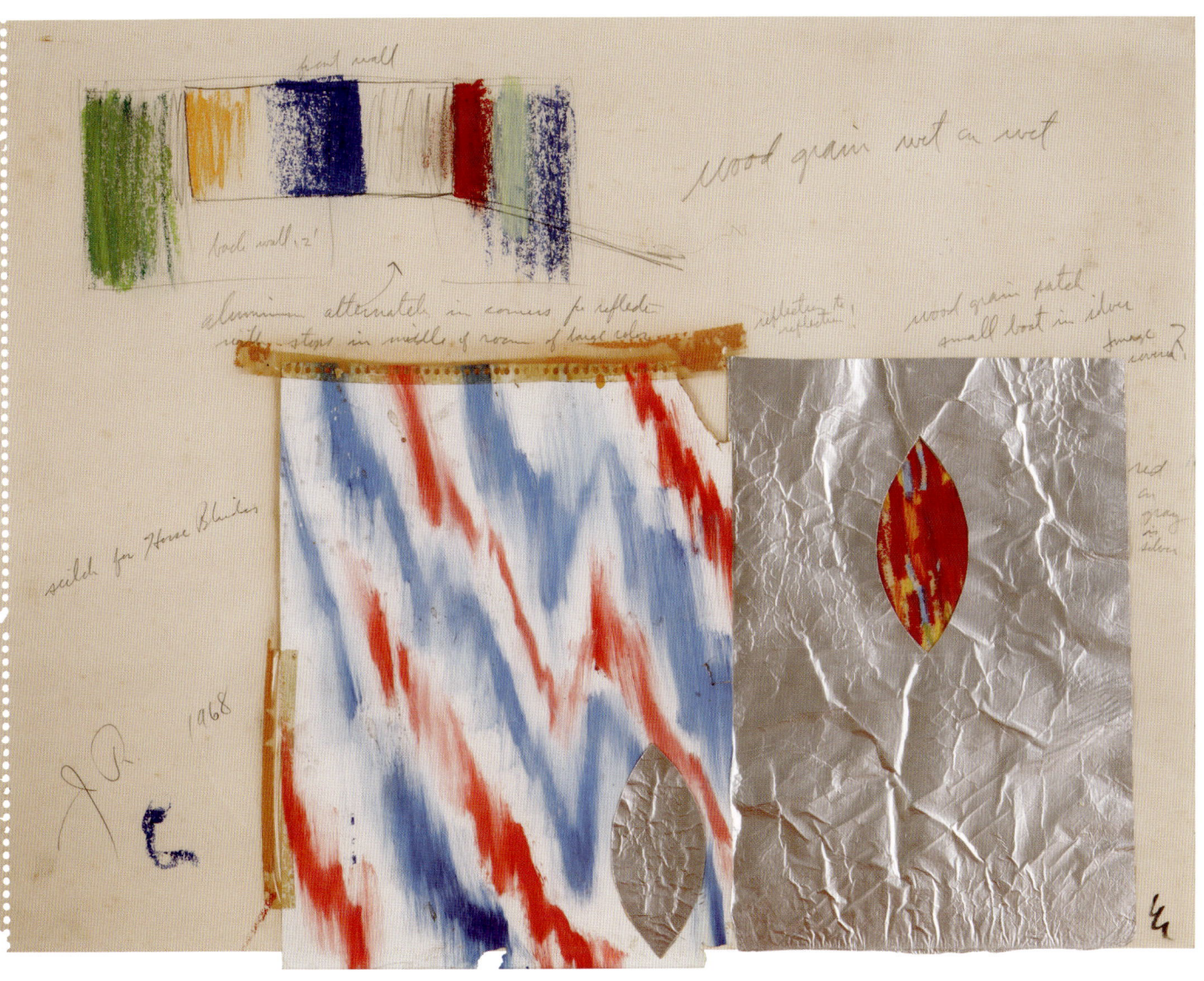

Sketch for Horse Blinders (Woodgrain Wet on Wet), 1968
Acrylic, crayon, graphite, foil, and collage on paper
18 1/4" x 23 3/4" (46.4 x 60.3 cm)
Private Collection

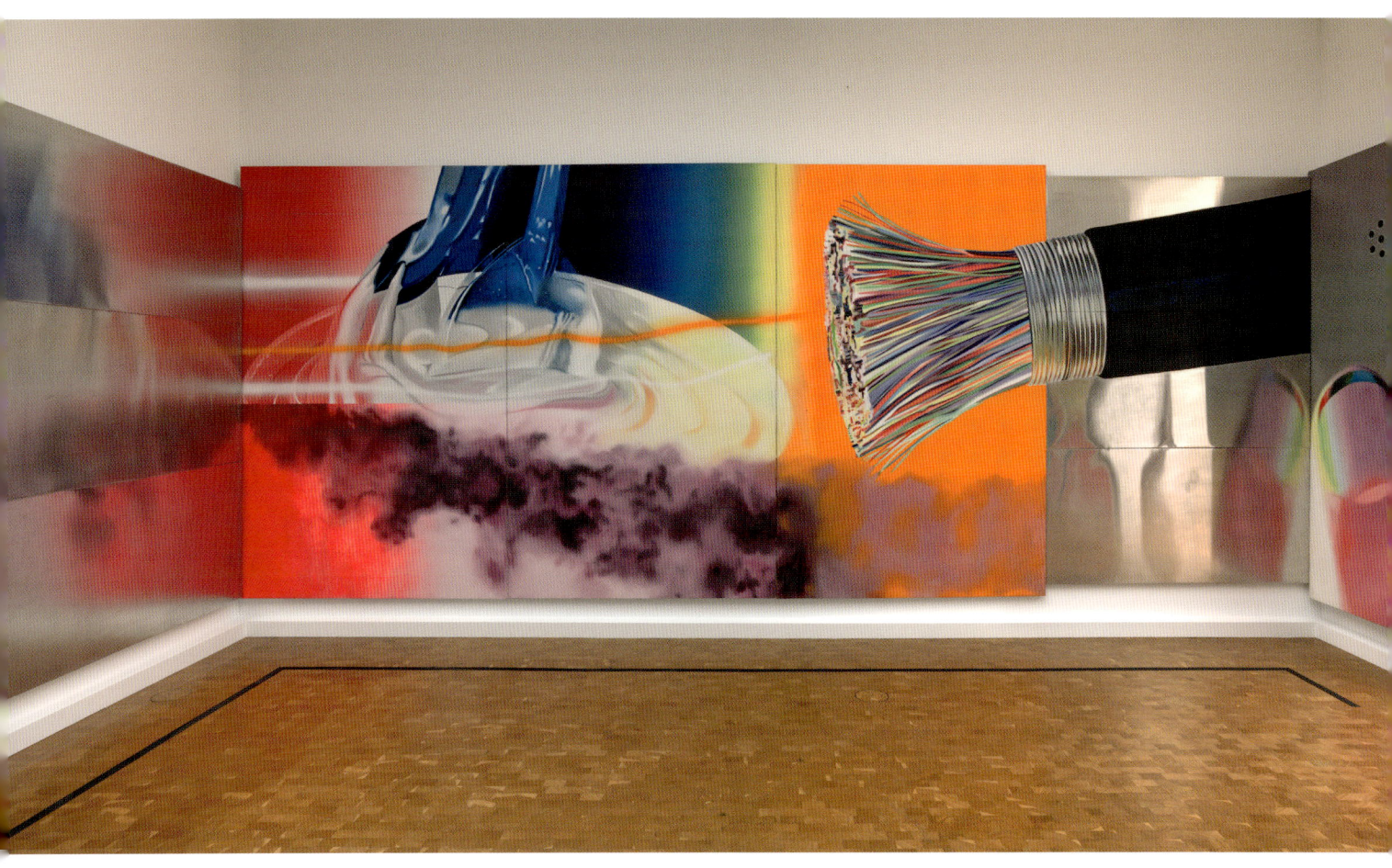

pages 94–97
Horse Blinders, 1968–69
Oil on canvas and aluminum (multipanel room installation)
10' x 84' 6" (304.8 x 2575.6 cm)
Collection of the Museum Ludwig, Cologne, Ludwig Donation, 1976 [ML 1121]

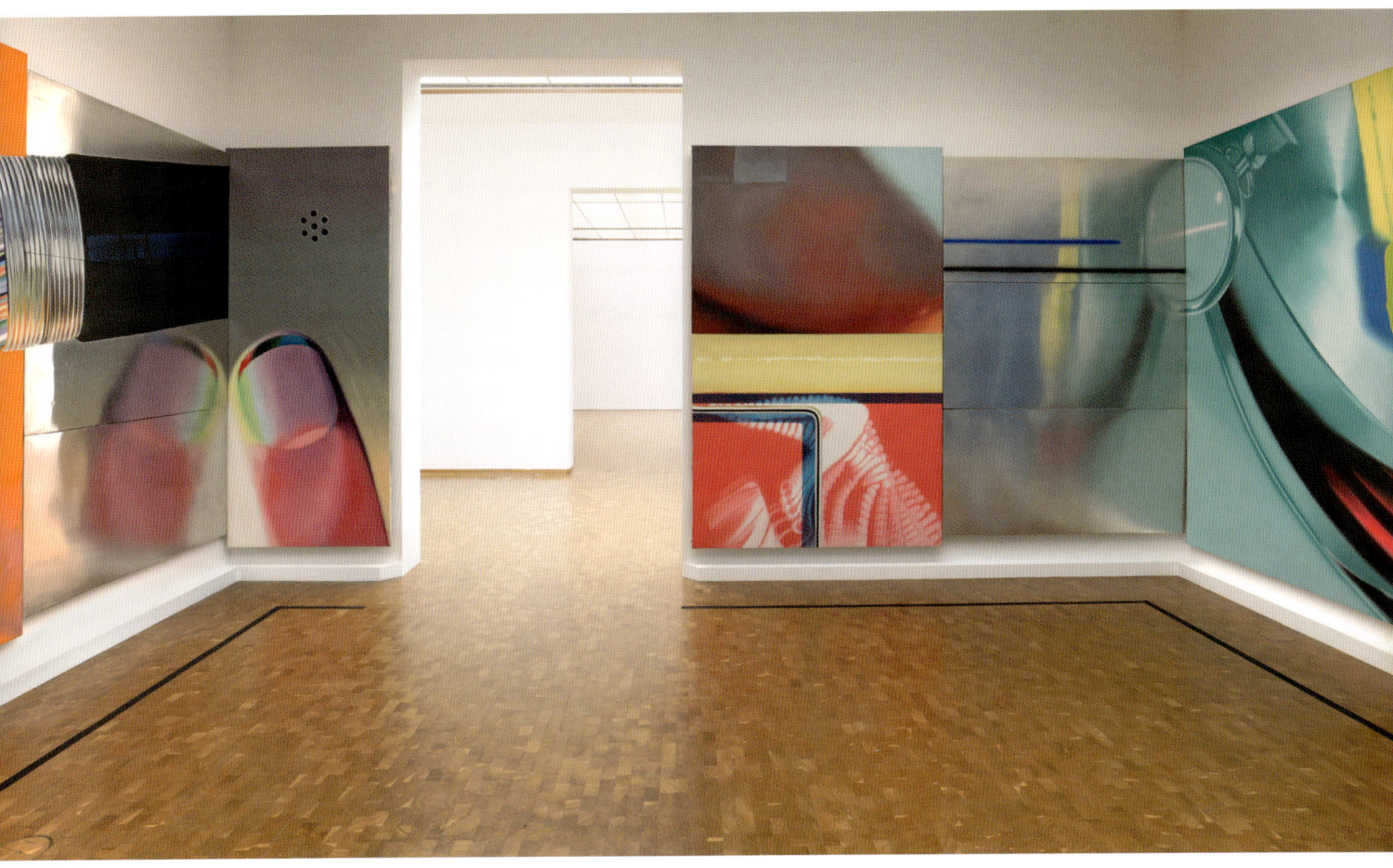

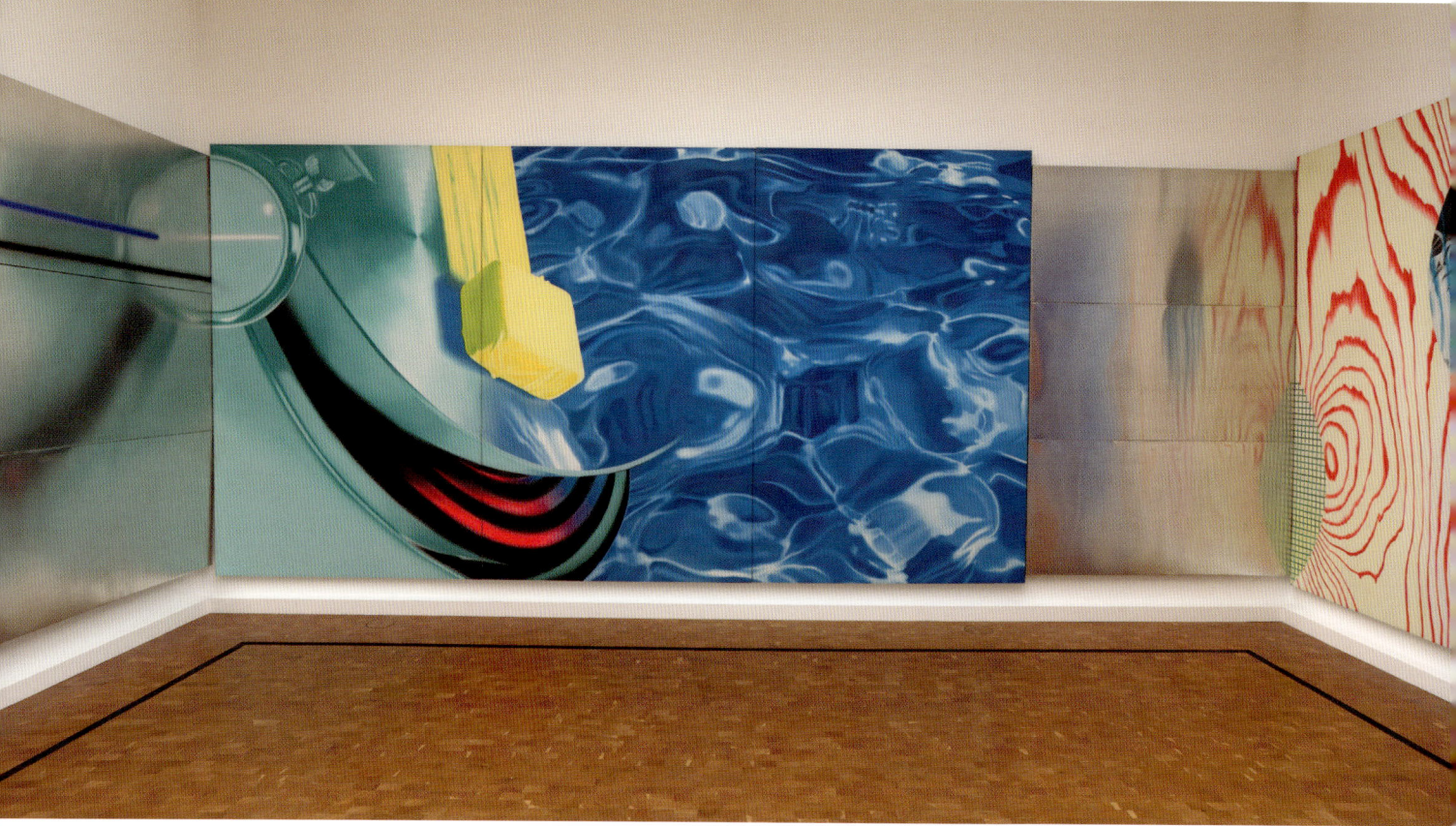

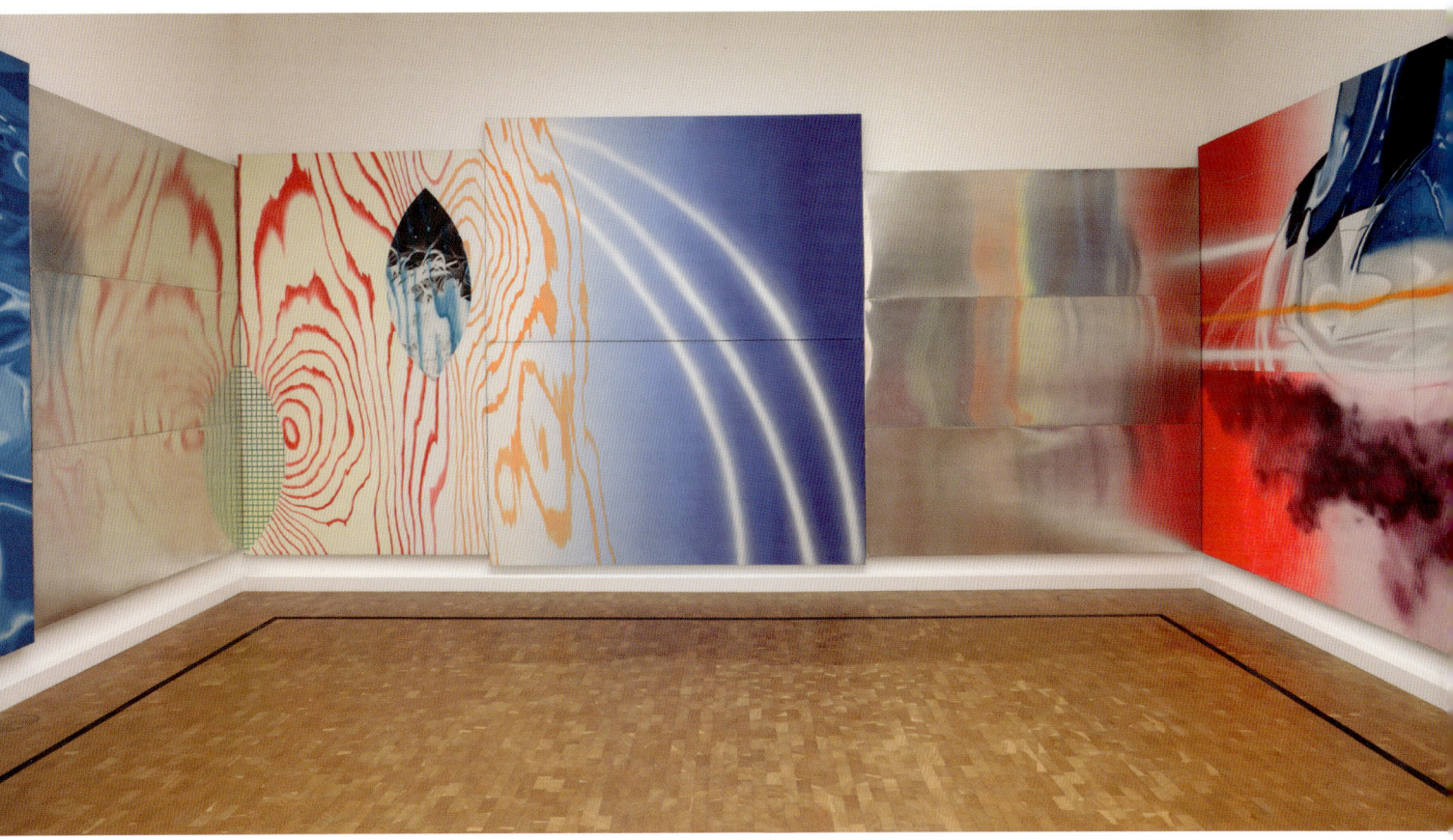

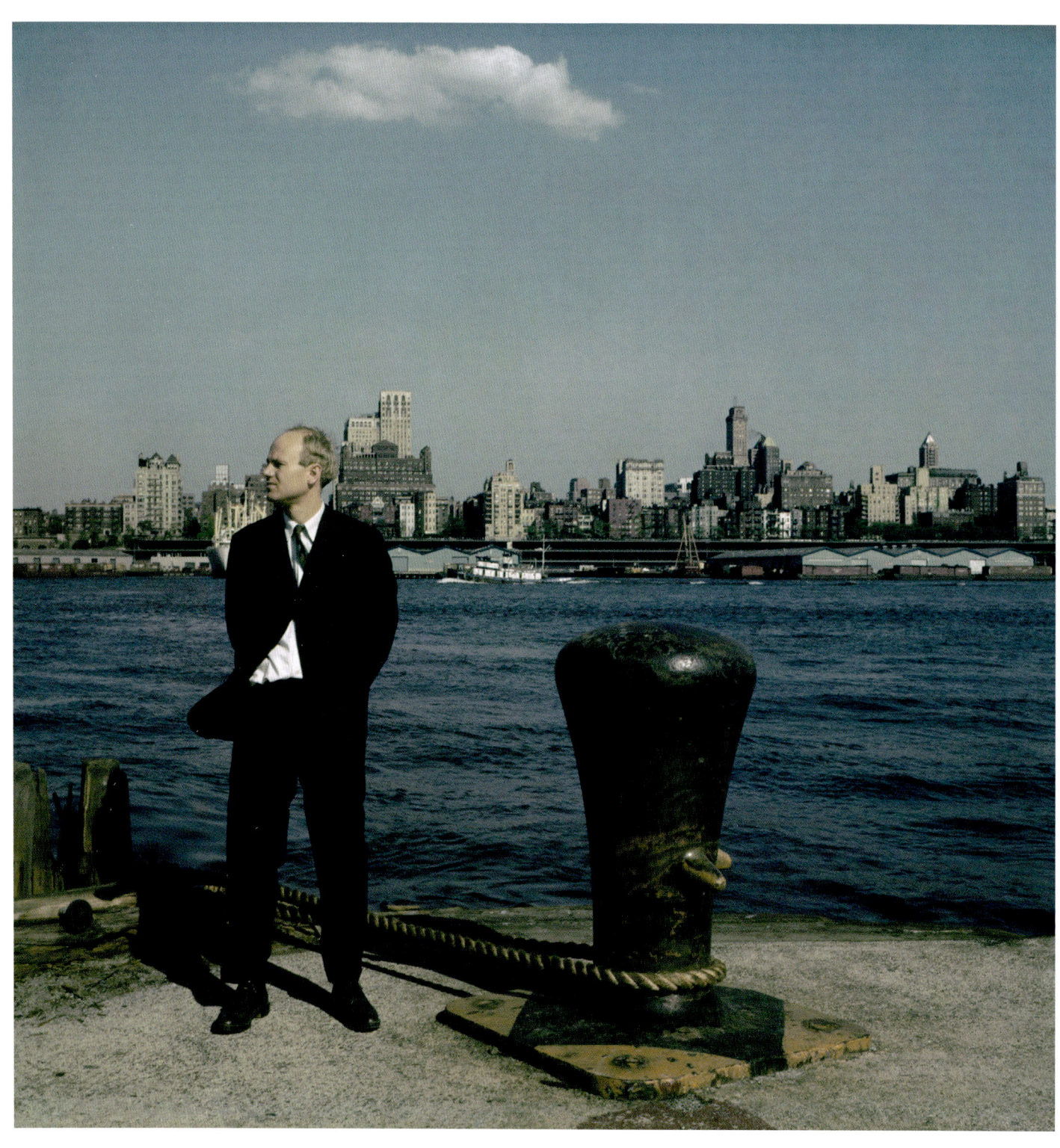

Rosenquist at Lower Manhattan's East River waterfront across from Brooklyn, New York, 1956.
Courtesy of the Estate of James Rosenquist

James Rosenquist

James Rosenquist (November 29, 1933–March 31, 2017) became well known in the 1960s as a leading American Pop artist alongside contemporaries Andy Warhol, Roy Lichtenstein, Claes Oldenburg, and other figurative artists. As with his contemporaries, Rosenquist's background in commercial art deeply influenced his nascent fine-art career. He and his Pop art colleagues radically influenced the course of modern art. While each Pop artist developed a distinct style, there were commonalities in their approaches to image-making that helped define the Pop art movement in the early 1960s: the use of commercial art techniques, and the depiction of popular imagery and everyday objects.

Drawing on his early experience as a billboard painter, Rosenquist culled imagery from print advertisements, photographs, and popular periodicals, recombining them to create mysterious and bold compositions. Utilizing the visual language of advertising in a style described by the late curator Walter Hopps as "visual poetry," Rosenquist's work has plumbed questions ranging from the economic, romantic, political, and ecological to the scientific, cosmic and existential. Over the course of his five-decade career, Rosenquist created seminal works in painting, drawing, collage, and printmaking. His art is included in major public and private institutions, and has been featured in solo exhibitions at the Solomon R. Guggenheim Museum, Museum of Modern Art, Walker Art Center, Whitney Museum of American Art, Guggenheim Museum Bilbao, Menil Collection, Museum of Fine Arts Houston, Denver Art Museum, Tretyakov Gallery, Museum Ludwig, Stedelijk Museum, and other national and international institutions.

Photo Credits

Page 5: Wolf P. Prange, ZADIK, H6, X, 1, Courtesy ZADIK Central Archive for German and International Art Market Research

Page 8: Ugo Mulas

Page 16: Glenn Steigelman, Courtesy of the Estate of James Rosenquist

Page 17: Peter Foe, Courtesy of the Estate of James Rosenquist

Page 19: Courtesy of the Estate of James Rosenquist

Page 22: Glenn Steigelman, Courtesy of the Estate of James Rosenquist

Page 23: George Holzer, Courtesy of the Estate of James Rosenquist

Page 25: Courtesy of the Estate of James Rosenquist

Page 29: Courtesy of Jack Shear Collection

Page 30: Glenn Steigelman, Courtesy of the Estate of James Rosenquist

Page 31: George Holzer, Courtesy of the Estate of James Rosenquist

Page 33: Courtesy of the Estate of James Rosenquist

Page 36: George Holzer, Courtesy of the Estate of James Rosenquist

Page 37: Courtesy of Private Collection

Page 39: Courtesy of Christie's, New York

Page 42: Glenn Steigelman, Courtesy of the Estate of James Rosenquist

Page 43: Peter Foe, Courtesy of the Estate of James Rosenquist

Page 45: Courtesy of the Estate of James Rosenquist

Page 48: Glenn Steigelman, Courtesy of the Estate of James Rosenquist

Page 49: Glenn Steigelman, Courtesy of the Estate of James Rosenquist

Page 50: Glenn Steigelman, Courtesy of the Estate of James Rosenquist

Page 51: Glenn Steigelman, Courtesy of the Estate of James Rosenquist

Page 52: Glenn Steigelman, Courtesy of the Estate of James Rosenquist

Page 53: Courtesy of the Estate of James Rosenquist

Page 56: Glenn Steigelman, Courtesy of the Estate of James Rosenquist

Page 57: George Holzer, Courtesy of the Estate of James Rosenquist

Pages 58–59: Courtesy of the Estate of James Rosenquist

Page 62: Glenn Steigelman, Courtesy of the Estate of James Rosenquist

Page 63: George Holzer, Courtesy of the Estate of James Rosenquist

Pages 64–65: Courtesy of the Estate of James Rosenquist

Page 68: Glenn Steigelman, Courtesy of the Estate of James Rosenquist

Page 69: George Holzer, Courtesy of the Estate of James Rosenquist

Page 71: Courtesy of the Estate of James Rosenquist

Pages 74–75: George Holzer, Courtesy of the Estate of James Rosenquist

Page 76: Russ Blaise, Courtesy of the Estate of James Rosenquist

Page 77: Russ Blaise, Courtesy of the Estate of James Rosenquist

Page 78: Russ Blaise, Courtesy of the Estate of James Rosenquist

Page 79: Russ Blaise, Courtesy of the Estate of James Rosenquist

Page 80: Russ Blaise, Courtesy of the Estate of James Rosenquist

Page 81: Russ Blaise, Courtesy of the Estate of James Rosenquist

Page 82: Glenn Steigelman, Courtesy of the Estate of James Rosenquist

Page 83: George Holzer, Courtesy of the Estate of James Rosenquist

Page 84: Courtesy of Christie's, New York

Page 85: Courtesy of the Estate of James Rosenquist

Page 86: George Hixson, Courtesy of Private Collection

Page 87: Courtesy of Bukowski Auktioner AB, Stockholm

Page 88: Courtesy of Private Collection

Page 89: Courtesy of the Estate of James Rosenquist

Page 90: Courtesy of the Estate of James Rosenquist

Page 91: Courtesy of the Estate of James Rosenquist

Page 92: Courtesy of the Estate of James Rosenquist

Page 93: Glenn Steigelman, Courtesy of the Estate of James Rosenquist

Pages 94–97: Britta Schlier, Courtesy of Rheinisches Bildarchiv Köln

Page 98: Courtesy of the Estate of James Rosenquist

Acknowledgments

First, my deepest thanks goes to the late James Rosenquist, and to Mimi Thompson Rosenquist and the James Rosenquist Estate, whose vision and collaboration brought this book into being. It is an honor to be aligned with such a legendary creative mind.

My gratitude to Sarah C. Bancroft, Head Curator of the James Rosenquist Estate, for her illuminating essay and many other contributions to this project. Thanks to Michael Harrigan and Lily Rosenquist for their work as well.

My profound appreciation goes as well to David Stark and the entire team at Artestar who facilitated the production of this publication. Special thanks to Sara Citarella.

My sincere appreciation, as always, to the entire team at Princeton University Press, especially Michelle Komie, Christie Henry, Terri O'Prey, Jacqueline Poirier, Colleen Suljic, Laurie Schlesinger, Cathy Felgar, Jodi Price, Kathryn Stevens, Annie Miller, Whitney Rauenhorst, and Mark Bellis. We remain extremely grateful to PUP for their continued professionalism, encouragement, and passion for our projects together throughout the years.

I would also like to acknowledge Brian Donnelly, John Pelosi, Angelo DiStefano, Mike Dean, Louise Donegan, Sickamore, Ferg, Keith Miller, and Sarah Sperling.

My special thanks in memoriam to Henry Geldzahler.

Very special thanks to Hannah Alderfer, Fiona Graham, and Susan Delson for their invaluable organization of this publication.

My sincere thanks to Taliesin Thomas for her amazing assistance on numerous projects, and to Steven Rodríguez for his continued support.

Finally, I give all my bottomless gratitude to my amazing wife, Abbey, and to my wonderful children, Justin, Ethan, Ellie, and Jonah for their love and encouragement.

As always, I give endless love and thanks to my mother Judith.

Larry Warsh

NO MORE RULERS (NMR) is on a mission to rethink the way we define art and creative expression. Based in New York, NMR is a publishing company dedicated to empowering the creative community and questioning the status quo. Our artist publications erase the boundaries between high and low, popular culture and fine art, and between traditional categories like design, music, and fashion. By partnering with global institutions and focusing on topics ranging from contemporary culture to artistic process to creativity, we're creating a world where art can truly be for everyone.

LARRY WARSH has been active in the art world for more than thirty years as a publisher and artist-collaborator. An early collector of Keith Haring and Jean-Michel Basquiat, Warsh was a lead organizer for the exhibition *Basquiat: The Unknown Notebooks*, which debuted at the Brooklyn Museum, New York, in 2015, and later traveled to several American museums. He also served as a curatorial consultant on *Keith Haring I Jean-Michel Basquiat: Crossing Lines* for the National Gallery of Victoria. The founder of Museums Magazine, Warsh has been involved in many publishing projects and is the editor of several other titles published by Princeton University Press, including *Basquiat-isms* (2019), *Haring-isms* (2020), *Futura-isms* (2021), *Abloh-isms* (2021), *Arsham-isms* (2021), *Warhol-isms* (2022), *Hirst-isms* (2022), *Pharrell-isms* (2023), *Judy Chicago-isms* (2023), *Holzer-isms* (2024), *Neshat-isms* (2024), *Jean-Michel Basquiat's The Notebooks* (2017), and *Keith Haring: 31 Subway Drawings* (2012), among others. Warsh has served on the board of the Getty Museum Photographs Council, and was a founding member of the Basquiat Authentication Committee until its dissolution in 2012.

NO MORE RULERS